BLAKE'S JOB

BLAKE'S JOB

A COMMENTARY

—

ANDREW WRIGHT

OXFORD
AT THE CLARENDON PRESS
1972

Oxford University Press, Ely House, London W. 1

GLASGOW NEW YORK TORONTO MELBOURNE WELLINGTON
CAPE TOWN IBADAN NAIROBI DAR ES SALAAM LUSAKA ADDIS ABABA
DELHI BOMBAY CALCUTTA MADRAS KARACHI LAHORE DACCA
KUALA LUMPUR SINGAPORE HONG KONG TOKYO

© OXFORD UNIVERSITY PRESS 1972

PRINTED IN GREAT BRITAIN
AT THE UNIVERSITY PRESS, OXFORD
BY VIVIAN RIDLER
PRINTER TO THE UNIVERSITY

FOR

MATTHEW AND EMMA

'A Spirit and a Vision are not, as the modern philosophy supposes, a cloudy vapour or a nothing: they are organized and minutely articulated beyond all that the mortal and perishing nature can produce. He who does not imagine in stronger and better lineaments, and in stronger and better light than his perishing mortal eye can see does not imagine at all.'

A Descriptive Catalogue

'If the doors of perception were cleansed every thing would appear to man as it is, infinite.'

The Marriage of Heaven & Hell

'Human nature is the image of God.'

Annotations to Lavater

'The whole Business of Man is the Arts & All Things Common.'

The Laocoön

PREFATORY NOTE

BLAKE'S most responsible critics have elucidated the Job Illustrations as they contribute to an understanding of the often puzzling myth that Blake constructed for himself out of disparate sources, the myth that forms the groundwork of his later poetry. Of course the context of Blake's reading and thinking and imagining must be taken into account at every point; the relationship exists and must be canvassed. But there is a danger too, the danger of burying the forest in the trees. However intimately related to the larger myth, the Job Illustrations must be comprehended as telling a story of their own, as all sensible men would agree. My study represents a different emphasis rather than a new departure.

Accordingly, the present work would have been inconceivable without its predecessors, especially the studies by Joseph Wicksteed, S. Foster Damon, Laurence Binyon and Sir Geoffrey Keynes, and Jean H. Hagstrum. An Appendix treats of their contributions in general; the notes record my indebtedness in detail, not only as a matter of scholarly propriety but also as a convenience to the reader, for whom I have recorded many variant interpretations. Thus besides elucidating each of the Illustrations in the main body of this book, I have provided, in one Appendix and in the notes, a kind of compendium of the commentary available, for those who want to weigh other possibilities.

Mr. P. G. Summers has kindly allowed his excellent set of the Illustrations to be reproduced here.

It is a pleasure to acknowledge my gratitude to the following persons who have provided help at various stages in the writing of this book: J. Bronowski, Martin Butlin, Thomas K. Dunsheath, David V. Erdman, Allen Fitchen, Sir Frank Francis, Sir Geoffrey Keynes, Douglas Matthews, Roy Harvey Pearce, Georgina Peyton, James Rupert, Barbara Schoneck, Wilbur Smith, Melvin Voigt, and Donald Wesling. A grant-in-aid from the University of California enabled me to go to London and study the Blake holdings in the British Museum and the Tate Gallery; to the generous-minded and knowledgeable staffs of these institutions I am grateful, as I have been for many years for various reasons.

The contributions of my students have been very helpful, in particular the

analyses by Jenijoy LaBelle of Blake's marginal texts, and the study by Robert
Essick of the artistic tradition to which Blake attached himself and which
nourished him. Robert Essick and Edward Howell also read versions of the
present study, as did my colleague Bram Dijkstra, himself a painter and poet.
These friends made valuable suggestions. Above all I am indebted to my old
teacher, M. O. Percival, who first introduced me to Blake's Job and who freely
shared his many fruitful ideas with me. Every page of the present study is
written in the light of the recoveries and discoveries of the foregoing—who
must not, however, be held accountable for any blunders or opacities which
may remain.

CONTENTS

ABBREVIATIONS   xiii

INTRODUCTION   xv

ILLUSTRATIONS OF THE BOOK OF JOB

Title-page   3

I	Job and his Family	5
II	Satan before the Throne of God	7
III	The Destruction of Job's Sons	11
IV	The Messengers tell Job of the Misfortunes that have Befallen him	15
V	Satan going forth from the Presence of the Lord	19
VI	Satan smiting Job with Boils	21
VII	Job's Comforters	23
VIII	Job's Despair	25
IX	The Vision of Eliphaz	27
X	Job rebuked by his Friends	29
XI	Job's Evil Dreams	31
XII	The Wrath of Elihu	33
XIII	The Lord answering Job out of the Whirlwind	35
XIV	The Creation	37
XV	Behemoth and Leviathan	39
XVI	The Fall of Satan	41
XVII	The Vision of God	43
XVIII	Job's Sacrifice	45
XIX	Job Accepting Charity	47
XX	Job and his Daughters	49
XXI	Job and his Wife restored to Prosperity	51

APPENDIX I. The Biblical Texts and Blake's Alterations   53

APPENDIX II. Previous Studies of the Job Illustrations   65

ABBREVIATIONS

B & K   Laurence Binyon and Geoffrey Keynes, eds., *The Illustrations of the Book of Job.* New York, 1935.

Damon   S. Foster Damon, *Blake's Job*. Providence, R.I., 1966.

Dict.   S. Foster Damon, *A Blake Dictionary*. Providence, R.I., 1965.

E   David V. Erdman, ed., *The Poetry and Prose of William Blake*. Garden City, N.Y., 1965. (Punctuation is occasionally, though sparingly, supplied by A. W. in the Job commentary.)

Hagstrum   Jean H. Hagstrum, *William Blake: Poet and Painter*. Chicago, 1964.

K   Geoffrey Keynes, ed., *The Complete Writings of William Blake with Variant Readings* (Oxford Standard Authors edition). London, 1966. This is a corrected reissue of the 1957 *Complete Writings* published by the Nonesuch Press.

Letters   Geoffrey Keynes, ed., *The Letters of William Blake*. 2nd ed. London, 1968.

Percival   M. O. Percival, *William Blake's Circle of Destiny*. New York, 1938.

Wicksteed   Joseph Wicksteed, *Blake's Vision of the Book of Job*. 2nd ed. London, 1924.

NOTE

The four epigraphs on p. vii can be found as follows: (1) E 532, K 576; (2) E 39, K 154; (3) E 586, K 83; (4) E 271, K 777.

INTRODUCTION

THE BOOK OF JOB raises the question of suffering and leaves it unanswered on the ground that God cannot be held accountable to man: the voice from the whirlwind comforts but does not enlighten Job, the just and upright man who has been made to suffer undeservingly. A patriarch without a past, he survives the several tests of his strength of faith and is rewarded not because he comprehends but because he endures.[1] To Blake, however, Job's failure to understand is rooted in an infirmity of imagination. Job is guilty of refusing to look, of contenting himself pridefully with a superficial apprehension of the world. The plot in Blake's version turns on the gradual revelation to Job that his supposition of innocence is itself rooted in ignorance: part of what Job is made to see is that he has been content to think of his outwardly observed pieties, his gestures of prayer and of charity, as indicative of genuine godliness; matched, in his patriarchal ascendancy and in his wealth, by divine manifestation of grace. Job has been living by the letter rather than by the spirit. So much he learns promptly—but so much is but half of what must be learned. When he comes to comprehend the meaning of true spirituality, when he discovers how to see not with but through the eye, he deserves and obtains the restoration of happiness depicted in the final Illustrations. Job's apocalypse—for it is nothing less— is of a divine humanity: irradiated by the force of imagination, enlightened by art, consoled and strengthened by love.

The *Illustrations of the Book of Job* mark the culmination of many years of meditation by Blake on the Old Testament tale. He published his great work in 1826 (the date on the label rather than that on the title-page is the correct one) and died in the following year, some three months before his seventieth birthday. But more than four decades earlier, when he was a young man of twenty-eight, Blake produced a pen-and-wash drawing of Job and his friends, a cruder version of Illustration X of the final series of engravings.[2] In the following

---

[1] See E. Dhorme, *A Commentary on the Book of Job*, trans. Harold Knight (London, 1967), pp. xv–xx, for an account of efforts to explain away or to invent a genealogy for Job.

[2] This drawing is now in the Tate Gallery. The assignment of 1785 as the date of composition is recorded in Geoffrey Keynes's 'The History of the "Job" Designs', Binyon and Keynes, *The*

years he turned again and again to the Book of Job, employing all the artistic means at his command—pencil, pen, brush, and burin—to capture the meaning which he sought to make the story express. But not until a few years before the Illustrations themselves were engraved did Blake put together a series of designs to the story as a whole. Sir Geoffrey Keynes hazards 1818 as the date of composition of the set of water-colour drawings which Blake's patron Thomas Butts bought from him. A set commissioned by Blake's young friend, the artist John Linnell—traced by Linnell and finished off in water-colour by Blake—was undertaken toward the end of 1821.[3] And Linnell later gave Blake the further commission, on very generous terms, of the engraved designs. These, the crowning achievement of Blake's distinguished career, are signally different from anything which preceded them: in none of the preliminary efforts is there border design or text, and Linnell described the borders as 'an afterthought'. Whether or not Linnell's report is correct, the fact is that—together with significant alterations in the Illustrations themselves—they make a narrative which simply did not come into existence until the series itself published in 1826 was completed.

Behind Blake's narrative lies the Book of Job, and Blake doubtless assumed that the reader would be struck by the contrasts in the two stories. Accordingly, one of the aims in the following pages is to consider Blake's narrative as it diverges from the Old Testament tale.[4] From the beginning a signal difference makes itself felt: Blake's Job and his God are identical. Job sees, that is he creates, God in his own image; this reversal is prefigured from the beginning, and it is patent throughout the series. Furthermore, Job's wife, unlike her Biblical counterpart, is prominent throughout the series and she is changeful:

Illustrations of the Book of Job (New York, 1935), to which I am indebted for many of the facts contained in this section of the introduction.

[3] The Butts water-colours (which, on internal evidence, Martin Butlin believes may be 'considerably earlier than 1818, perhaps nearer 1810') are now in the Pierpont Morgan Library in New York. Eighteen of the Linnell set of drawings are at the Fogg Art Museum at Harvard. A series of pencil sketches, which mark a stage in the conversion of the water-colours to engraved prints, is in the Fitzwilliam Museum in Cambridge. The New Zealand set, so called because they were discovered in Auckland in 1928, having been

brought there by a pupil of Linnell's, also mark a transition between the large water-colours and the engravings. These water-colours are in the collection of Mr. Paul Mellon. These three preliminary versions of the engraved designs, together with a number of the pencil sketches and the 1826 Illustrations themselves, have been reproduced in a splendid portfolio edited by Laurence Binyon and Geoffrey Keynes (New York, 1935). See Appendix II to the present study.

[4] This approach itself has a history. It may be traced in Keynes's *Blake Studies* (London, 1949), pp. 146-8.

she is depicted not objectively but as Job sees her. Finally, there is the theme of vision, that of seeing with the inward eye. Of this, more will be said at the proper place; for the time being it may be enough to assert that Blake's Job story is unfolded entirely from the viewpoint of the hero: the Illustrations have what Henry James later was to call a 'commanding centre'. They therefore have a coherence of a different order from that found in the Old Testament version—and a different force, and a different meaning.[5]

The importance of the marginal texts can hardly be exaggerated, but their full impact can be felt only in the context of Blake's absorbed and supple knowledge of the Old and New Testaments. Many of these texts are from the Book of Job itself, but some are not. In his designs Blake draws on a close acquaintance with the whole of the Bible, and he engraves texts from Genesis to Revelation. An Appendix to the present study identifies these marginalia, but such a map gives nothing more than an indication of the quality and significance of Blake's choices. There is another point to be noticed as well, namely that Blake often alters the Biblical texts, turning the phraseology of the Authorized Version to suit the meaning which he intends to embody. All in all the use of the Bible by Blake points to a confidence which signalizes great originality, and substantially incorporates a new version of the story of Job.

Besides the Book of Job itself there is another context that must be kept in mind by the reader of Blake's narrative. This is the tradition within which Blake wrote—the 'other tradition', as it has been called, the heterodox strain ranging from the Orphic mysteries of the sixth century before Christ to the writings of Emmanuel Swedenborg in the eighteenth century. Blake's mythology, as more and more readers have come to realize, is neither the chaotic—or merely private—piecework of a madman (although that 'tradition' has died hard), nor the idiosyncratic construction of an autodidact whose impatience with earlier formulations caused him to jettison them altogether. Blake's myth, or system, is deeply traditional, and yet it is his in that he made a synthesis which is defiantly his own. In the prophecies he rehearses, with sometimes strident insistence, the fall into disintegration. Again and again he writes of the separation

---

[5] Wicksteed's own effort is more detailed and schematic than mine. 'Job's error', he says, 'was his boasted perfection. For the individual to be fortified with every outward and even inward good is not, as he supposes, to cut himself off from evil, but to cut himself off from an infinite good, which he can find only in a deep sense of imperfection and in the divine society of Man. This alone is Paradise, whether in earth or heaven' (pp. 77-8). See also Appendix II to the present study.

of the whole man, whom he calls Albion, into the four 'living creatures':
Urthona (or Los), representing the imagination; Luvah, representing emotion;
Urizen, representing reason; Tharmas, representing the physical body—and
of the 'emanations' from each of them of the corresponding female figures
Enitharmon, Vala, Ahania, and Enion. The myth is Blake's own compound,
but it is deeply indebted to neo-Platonic, Gnostic, Cabbalistic, and other
heterodox doctrines. Because other critics have already covered this ground
very thoroughly, I do not intend to rehearse their work here.[6] Nor do I think
it centrally relevant to a study of the Job Illustrations.

Because the framework of Blake's conception of the universe is symbolic,
and because Blake refuses to employ a generally accessible symbolic apparatus,
his readers have had to learn the new language which he put together out of
a lifetime of contemplation not only of the Bible and Milton but also the repre-
sentatives of the 'other tradition', Emmanuel Swedenborg especially.[7] But in

[6] The other tradition has been examined by such diverse critics as S. Foster Damon, *William Blake, His Philosophy and Symbols* (Boston, Mass., 1924); M. O. Percival, *William Blake's Circle of Destiny* (New York, 1938); Northrop Frye, *Fearful Symmetry* (Princeton, N.J., 1947); Harold Bloom, *Blake's Apocalypse* (Garden City, N.Y., 1963); Desirée Hirst, *Hidden Riches* (London, 1964); and by Kathleen Raine, *Blake and Tradition* (2 vols., Princeton, N.J., 1968).

[7] Emmanuel Swedenborg (1688-1772), the scientist-turned-mystic whom Blake admired but whom he came to criticize bitterly, had much in common with his spiritual forebears, Boehme especially. Most notably his theology is mono-theistic, and Jesus is the one God, 'Divinity and Humanity being one Person' (*Divine Providence*, n. 22). Swedenborg is important for his doctrine of correspondences, the theory that the natural world provides material symbols of the spiritual realities in eternity: the whole natural world corre-sponds 'to the spiritual world; not only generally, but in detail. Whatever comes forth in the natural world from the spiritual, is therefore called corre-spondent. The world of nature comes forth and subsists from the spiritual world, just as an effect does from its efficient cause' (*Heaven and Hell*, n. 89). Blake took over the doctrine in the large, though not in detail. But when in *A Vision of the Last Judgment* Blake gives his own prescription for seeing, he is being eminently Swedenborgian. 'I assert for My self that I do not behold the Out-ward Creation & that to me it is hindrance & not Action; it is as the Dirt upon my feet, No part of Me. "What," it will be Questiond, "When the Sun rises, do you not see a round Disk of fire somewhat like a Guinea?" O no no, I see an Innumerable company of the Heavenly host cry-ing "Holy, Holy, Holy is the Lord God Almighty". I question not my corporeal or Vegetative Eye any more than I would Question a Window concerning a Sight. I look thro' it & not with it' (E 555, K 617). None the less, there are Swedenborgian doctrines that Blake abhorred, in particular Swedenborg's dualism, and, as is well known, Blake held Swedenborg up to contemptuous scorn in *The Marriage of Heaven and Hell*. But Blake's rejection of Swedenborg is more notorious than the extent of his indebtedness to him, and it is well to underscore the fact that the influence was pervasive, in part because Swedenborg's thought sums up so much of the 'other tradition'. Above all, Blake's religion is Swedenborgian in its inward-ness. Blake's religion, as Professor Percival remarks, 'has no outward ceremonial. Its worship consists in honoring the imagination in whatever human breast it happens to reside.' (Percival, p. 129.)

the Job series it is necessary to have in mind little more than the broad outlines
of the shifting fable which can be traced in its mutations and permutations in
the prophetic books, early and late. The re-casting of the Book of Job provides
the necessary and proper focus. 'All that we See is vision', Blake wrote in *The
Laocoön*,[8] and when we, like Job, have learned to look, the story of the *Illustrations of the Book of Job* tells itself. Seeing is understanding—but to see clearly
is not easy. 'For the work of the greatest artists', in the fine words of Northrop
Frye, 'begins in an attempt to make the appearance real, and ends in an attempt
to make reality appear. The assumption underlying art, then, is that the natural
world is related to the mental world as material is related to form, diversity to
unity, the analytic to the synthetic aspect of the same thing.'[9]

That Blake's myth alters from prophecy to prophecy has annoyed some
readers and misled some critics; but Blake grew, changed, developed, as do all
human beings who do not, for one reason or another, arrest and therefore
stultify the creative impulse within them. In *Vala*, in *Milton*, and in *Jerusalem*
Blake writes of creation, fall, suffering, apocalypse, redemption. Behind these
works lies a consistent vision of life that can be stated simply. 'First', in the
words of Professor Percival,

it is a life lived from within. These alone are the vision, the faith, the energy, the capacity
for self-sacrifice, by means of which Jerusalem can be built. It cannot be built by the
virtues which reside in the outward principle, in distrust or denial of these inward virtues. Reason divorced from faith and intuition; emotions, well-intentioned, perhaps, but
ungrounded in the higher intelligence which alone can render them effective; the selfishness of the natural man not broken and transmuted by the divine vision of all men as
brothers—these faculties will not suffice. This is the essence of the Blakean message.[10]

Such is the groundwork of Blake's myth, but its translation into fable brought
difficulties which were sometimes insuperable. All his life Blake endeavoured
to marry poetry and picture, and his work in what he called illuminated print-
ing stands as a unique but uneven achievement. The *Songs of Innocence* (1789)
and the *Songs of Experience* (1794) are perfect; the early prophecies—from
Tiriel (1789) through *The Book of Los* (1795)—are exquisite though occasionally misty.[11] The three later prophecies are longer, more ambitious, more fully

[8] E 271, K 776.
[9] Frye, op. cit., p. 384.
[10] Percival, p. 279.
[11] The very complex Blake chronology is treated authoritatively by G. E. Bentley, Jr., in his *Blake Bibliography* (Minneapolis, Minn., 1964), pp. 31-8. The co-editor of this volume is Martin K. Nurmi.

realized. But *Vala* (1795–1808), *Milton* (1801–8), and *Jerusalem* (1804–20) present extremely vexed challenges of various kinds. *Vala* is a series of false starts and was never arranged in final form. The title-page of *Milton* announces a poem in twelve books; only two appear to have been engraved. *Jerusalem* was indeed completed, but it is a vast puzzle, oracular and opaque; at least no one, not even Northrop Frye, has been able to provide a reading that clarifies more than a few of the positively fearful ambiguities and inconsistencies of that resistant masterpiece. And *Jerusalem*'s very order seems never to have been definitively worked out by the author.[12] The sacrifice of narrative continuity exacts a high price.

It is certainly true that Blake's view of human destiny altered not merely from youth to maturity but from one mature work to another. *Milton* and *Jerusalem* tell the same story but the versions are different enough—and dark enough—to make the reader know that Blake was working toward a statement that eventually he found himself unable to formulate within the framework of the 'system' that he invented. Such, at least, is my view, and I do not for a moment suppose that it will find favour everywhere. Let it therefore be regarded as speculation and treated as the dispensable opinion of one reader of Blake. But it is certainly true that in his last years Blake no longer attempted to tell his story in his own words. He turned to Job (and also to Dante), and it is my argument that the Job Illustrations say lucidly what Blake had been trying to say all along.[13] While it is both useful and necessary to consider Blake's Job in the light of his earlier achievements, it is a mistake to read into the Illustrations the symbols of the prophetic books, at least at their earlier valuations.

The tale of Job as Blake tells it is classically simple. In part the story is of the fall—into selfhood, into division, into sexuality. The fall is also outward, from inwardness and spirituality into materiality. But that is only half the tale, as the circle of destiny on the title-page of the Job series shows. The remainder of Job's story is a renewal of what has been lost, after the Last Judgement which measures every individual. Innocence gives way to experience, but experience

---

[12] There are five complete copies known. Professor Erdman calls the arrangement of the plates 'inconstant', but there is variation only in Chapter 2. 'After two copies in the same order, Blake printed two in a variant order . . . and then returned to the first. Evidently he found both sequences, attractive but considered neither definitive' (E 370).

[13] No one is more lucid on the relationship of Blake's myth to the Job Illustrations than Professor Percival, pp. 138–9.

itself prefigures the redemption that completes the circle and fulfils the destiny of mankind.

As a human being Job belongs to the race of Adam and is therefore fallen. To Blake Job is a man of intellect, far superior to his wife and to the friends who accuse him. But he has allowed his mind to separate itself from the indispensable considerations of inwardness that are the conditions of grace. The divorce between inward and outward has led to what might be called a spectrous misconception, that materiality can give accurate information about his spiritual condition. Job is doubly fallen in that he has allowed reason to triumph over imagination. It is an elementary mistake, in Blake's view, to suppose that health and wealth are manifestations of divine favour. It is to misconceive the meaning of incarnation—'the hint half guessed, the gift half understood', in Eliot's words[14]—and to this central concept Blake attaches a special importance. Job's neglect of art is a negation of spiritual manifestation; his redemption is signalized in the two concluding Illustrations, when he himself makes a work of art—he tells his own story to his daughters—and when, at last, the musical instruments are employed rather than eschewed. The story and the music are certainly joyous, for they tell of a salvation that takes place in this world. They tell of the paradise within.

[14] 'The Dry Salvages', in *Four Quartets* (New York, 1943), p. 27.

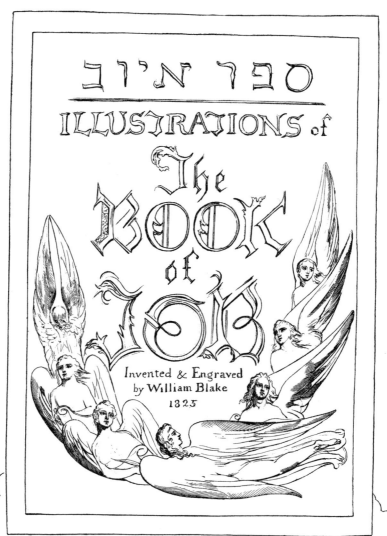

ספר איוב

ILLUSTRATIONS of

The BOOK of JOB

Invented & Engraved
by William Blake
1825

London Published as the Act directs March 8:1825. by William Blake Nº 3 Fountain Court Strand

Title-page

Blake proclaims his independence of the eighteenth century in the anti-classical lettering on the title-page: the Hebrew letters (saying 'Book of Job') and the Gothic letters in which the English words are engraved are both—by their very design—declarations of freedom. Blake turns his back on the Augustan tradition into which he was born and undertakes in the Job Illustrations to cleanse the doors of perception, to show the realities behind—or rather within—the merely natural world, the realities which the natural world both presages and contains.

The seven angels are here seen to be tracing a circle of destiny anticipating the narrative itself. In this way Blake makes a radical claim and a fresh start. The emphasis which in the Biblical version falls on Job's trial shifts to a sense of completion foreshadowed by the pictorial allusion to the seven eyes of God in the Book of Revelation[1] and by the depiction of the figure of Jesus:[2] by Blake's theology the fall is downward and outward; the return, upward and inward. Taken in Blake's explicit terms—'What is Above is Within'[3]—the story of Job is thus declared to be one of inner experience, for Jesus is inward-turning in this design. But Blake faces directly the paradox of incarnation—he accepts the embodiment which the circle of destiny illustrates. He does not renounce the flesh. Inwardness for Blake always depends on physical manifestation. Accordingly, while Job's trial is to be essentially of the spirit, Blake will show the relationship between physique and essence. The fact that three of the angels hold scrolls[4] (and that one holds a quill): these signify creative expression and prefigure redemption. Art shows the way. Early in his career, in *The Marriage of Heaven and Hell*, Blake put into Ezekiel's mouth the following words: 'We of Israel taught that the Poetic Genius . . . was the first principle and all others merely derivative, which was the cause of our despising the Priests & Philosophers of other countries, and prophecying that all Gods would at last be proved to originate in ours & to be the tributaries of the Poetic Genius.'[5] Altogether, the title-page can be considered as a manifestation of the double sense in which Blake regards creation, and what appears at first to be contradictory is reconciled in the engraving. The clockwise direction[6] of the angels is regarded by Blake as the current of creation itself, that is, from east to west. It is downward into experience and upward toward redemption. But artistic expression, as signified by the quill, is only possible when manifested in the realm of experience: art is incarnation.

---

[1] Damon asserts that the seven eyes represent the 'whole course of human thought in its search for an ideal by which to live' (Damon, p. 4).

[2] The angels are named by Blake elsewhere (*Vala*, Night VIII (E 366, K 351); *Milton*, Pl. 13. 17–27 (E 106, K 494); *Jerusalem*, Pl. 55. 30–2 (E 202, K 686)). Cf. Rev. 5: 6: 'the seven eyes, which are the seven Spirits of God sent forth into all the earth'.

[3] *Jerusalem*, Pl. 71. 6 (E 222, K 709).

[4] 'The contrast between the books of Law and the scrolls of Inspiration is carried through from the first illustration to the last' (Damon, p. 4). Wicksteed does not make this distinction.

[5] *The Marriage of Heaven and Hell* (E 38, K 153).

[6] Wicksteed, p. 87. This is one of his most important *aperçus*. Cf. *Jerusalem*, Pl. 77. 4–5 (E 230, K. 717). Damon writes that the descent and ascent of the angels here corresponds to 'the underground course of the sun, which sets in Illustrations I–VII but rises again in Illustration XXI' (Damon, p. 10).

Our Father which art in Heaven   hallowed be thy Name

Thus did Job continually

There was a Man in the
Land of Uz whose Name
was Job. & that Man
was perfect & upright

The Letter Killeth
The Spirit giveth Life

It is Spiritually Discerned

& one that feared God
& eschewed Evil & there
was born unto him Seven
Sons & Three Daughters

WBlake inv & sculp

London. Published as the Act directs. March 8: 1828. by Will™ Blake N 3 Fountain Court Strand.

I Job and his Family

The apparent serenity of the scene depicted in the design is precarious and superficial. Job and his family are gathered beneath the central tree in postures of satisfaction, of self-satisfaction with a life that is patently outward and material. All appear to be praying, to be observing the proprieties. The text immediately beneath the central design is 'Thus did Job continually'—referring to the burnt offerings made—'continually'—by Job on behalf of his sons who may 'have sinned and cursed God in their hearts'. That observance of the forms of prayer is inadequate is indicated by the connection established between the books on the laps of Job and his wife, the text from the Book of Job, and the words from Corinthians on the altar in the lower border: 'The Letter Killeth. The Spirit giveth Life. It is Spiritually Discerned.' Nor should the first words of the Lord's Prayer be regarded as marking merely the beginning of Blake's story. Job's prayer-ful utterances are the vain repetitions spoken of in the same chapter of Saint Matthew that also contains the instructions for prayer, including the Lord's Prayer itself; and this chapter contains the following injunction as well: 'Lay not up for yourselves treasures upon earth, where moth and rust doth corrupt, and where thieves break through and steal.'[1] In the corresponding chapter in Luke, the Pharisees are rebuked for outward observance, 'but your inward part is full of ravening and wickedness'.[2]

Blake's Job is not perfect and upright, but he is blind enough to imagine himself to be so; and the opening words of the Book of Job, engraved here in the lower border, become the more deeply ironic as the design is comprehended. For the reader, unlike Job, can see that much is amiss. The sun is setting behind a Gothic cathedral that is removed from the devotions. The musical instruments hang unused, among them the timbrel and harp spoken of bitterly by the Biblical Job as the pastimes of the wicked.[3] The sacrificial lambs on the altar in the lower border are also portentous, especially in view of the words which appear on the altar itself, for they must stand as the indictment to be laid against Job. The first signs of the Zodiac, the ram and the bull, appear here in reverse order—that is, out of order. Inevitably the scene as a whole takes on the look of impending disaster or doom—or both. This fact is emphasized by the ambiguous appearance of one of the sheep in the very centre of the lower part of the design: the sheep resembles a dog, emblematic of accusation throughout the Bible: Job himself speaks contemptuously of those 'whose fathers I would have disdained to have set with the dogs of my flock'.[4]

The tree in this Illustration provides a focus and a double meaning. To Job, as the story is being told from his viewpoint, the tree is symbolically ameliorative—the tree of life. To the reader observing the many evidences of disharmony, disunity, disorder in the Illustration, the tree looks to have a falsely comforting aspect—the tree of mystery. This accords with the ambiguity of the symbol both in the Bible and in Blake.[5]

Behind the tree are many sheep, a traditional

---

[1] Matt. 6:19.

[2] Luke 11:19.

[3] Job 21:12.

[4] Job 30:1. Blake attaches pejorative connotations to dogs elsewhere in his work as well. There is, for instance, a grim and lethal-looking dog-like animal in the water-colour *Plague*, reproduced as Pl. 38a in *William Blake's Illustrations to the Bible*, ed. Geoffrey Keynes (London, 1957). Compare *Vala*, Night II. 389-90: '"I have chosen the serpent for a councellor, and the dog / For a schoolmaster to my children"' (E 318, K 290). On the curious appearance of the animal depicted by Blake, the point should be made that the eighteenth century saw spectacular improvement in the breeding of sheep and oxen, owing to the efforts of Robert Bakewell (1725-95): 'He changed English sheep, from the resemblance of a cross between a dog and a goat, to the plump, fleece-covered animal we know today.' (J. H. Plumb, *England in the Eighteenth Century* [London, 1950], p. 83.)

[5] The range in the Bible is from the tree of knowledge in Genesis to the tree of life in the Book of Revelation. In Blake there is 'the eternal Oak' of *The Book of Los* (E 89, K 256) as well as 'a Tree of Misery' composed of 'Good & Evil [which] are Riches & Poverty' in *The Laocoön* (E 270-1, K 776) and the deadly tree of Moral Virtue in *Jerusalem*, Pl. 28. 15 (E 172, K 652). 'What Blake means by Mystery . . . is a religion of externalities and ceremonies' (Percival, p. 34). This is precisely what Job has made of religion.

sign of wealth. Likewise there are tents of prosperity beneath the star and moon, and a tent enclosing the design as a whole. The reader of Blake's poetry is at this point reminded of the heart-felt cry in *Vala*:

It is an easy thing to rejoice in the tents of prosperity,
Thus could I sing & thus rejoice, but it is not so with me![6]

Although this Illustration marks the beginning of the story as Blake is to tell it, the narrative may be said to begin *in medias res*, and in a different way from that of the Biblical narrative.[7] The Book of Job opens with a portrait of perfection. What compels attention is the spectacle of a series of undeserved misfortunes visited upon a good man who clings to his faith despite the severest trials. Blake's Job, however, is deluded by his material possessions, by his comfortable family circle, and by the superficial pieties with which he pays lip service to the spirit that giveth life. The Biblical Job is perfect and upright. Blake's Job is a sinner, the victim of a failure of perception: what Blake calls 'single vision'. The setting sun, the rising moon, and the single star in the design are indicative of Job's infirmity. 'May God us keep', Blake pleads in a letter to Thomas Butts, 'From Single vision & Newton's sleep.'[8]

---

[6] E 319, K 291.
[7] Damon, however, declares that 'Job and his family are still in the pastoral state of innocence' (Damon, p. 12). My view on the other hand, is that Job mistakenly supposes himself to be in that state.
[8] E 693, K 818.

II. SATAN BEFORE THE THRONE OF GOD
overleaf

I shall see God

We shall awake up

I beheld the

Hast thou considered my Servant Job

Ancient of Days

The Angel of the Divine Presence

מלך יהוה

Thou art our Father

in thy Likeness

W Blake inv & sc

When the Almighty was yet with me, When my Children were about me

There was a day when the Sons of God came to present themselves before the Lord & Satan came also among them. to present himself before the Lord

London Published as the Act directs March 8: 1825 by Will.m Blake N 3 Fountain Court Strand.

II Satan before the Throne of God

A diminished patriarch makes his appearance here. Job and his family are literally oppressed, chiefly— perhaps wholly—by the constructs of his own diseased imagination. No longer the law-abiding citizen who has been able to congratulate himself on his riches, his family life, and his piety, Job becomes anxious, and—even among his wife and children—isolated. His right hand is drawn away from the shoulder of his wife; he does not respond to the pressure of his son's nearness: he is grasping a book. In the centre of the design Satan is running in sheets of flame—youthful and full of energy, arms raised in appeal to the figure of God above. Job acknowledges though he does not want to countenance Satan's penetration of his horrid and yet still tidy imaginings. For here is Job's God, counterpart of the figure at the bottom of the design: it is God created by Job in his own image. He is upon a Druidical seat holding a book containing the letter that killeth, the law of sacrifice. In Blake's mind there is a constant association of blood sacrifice and Druidic religious practice; consequently, Druid symbols, which abound in the Job series, always have a pejorative connotation, not because they are unchristian, but because they are associated with murder. The expression of weariness, of readiness to be defeated, in God's eyes, the blankness of his look, the feebleness with which he points with his right hand (or allows it to hang aimlessly), as evidently he addresses Satan with the words from the Book of Job, 'Hast thou considered my servant Job', all point to the disquiet felt by Job himself, even though he regards himself as a man 'the Almighty was yet with'—for these two texts are engraved in the upper and lower borders respectively.

Around the figure of God are, including Satan, the seven angels who appear first on the Title-page. At least two of them are depositing scrolls at the feet of God who, as the image of Job, becomes the lawgiver. This surrender of the emblems of artistic instinct[1] represents an acquiescence in the schemes of the Angel of the Divine Presence who is Satan, the Jehovah of law and sacrifice explicitly associated by Blake with Satan in the upper border of this Illustration, where the Hebrew words 'Jehovah is king' appear immediately below the words 'The Angel of the Divine Presence'.[2]

Two fairly obscure heads, disembodied shadows of Job and his wife,[3] appear in a background of flame; already Job half recognizes that he has been enthralled by Satan. Three figures, who may be Job's daughters, are next to Satan, significant here as prefiguring the three daughters to whom Job will tell his tale in Illustration XX, once the circle of destiny is complete.

In the lower section of the design—where nearly 'every figure . . . is provided with a book of "the letter that killeth"'[4]—Job and his wife sit, again beneath the tree, again holding books. There are but six children here. Two scroll-bearing angels ('whose wings faintly suggest Sinaitic tablets')[5] hover by Job's wife, on her right hand, directly in front of a number of sheep—significantly, however, not so many as in Illustration I. A dog, this time definitely a dog, is lying beneath the bench, on Job's left.[6] One of Job's sons is standing and holding an open book, his left foot on the ground, his right heel resting on a book beneath the bench.

There are three trees in this design. The trunks are entwined with creepers or serpents. The tree furthest to the right, as one looks at the design, has

---

[1] Here I part company with Wicksteed, who declares that the resemblance of God and man is founded on the possession by them both of identical poetic genius. Cf. Wicksteed, p. 93. My own view, consonant in this respect with that of Damon, remains closer to observation of the Illustration.

[2] The connection is made also in *A Vision of the Last Judgment* (E 549, K 610). And here it may be useful to refer to Wicksteed's discovery of—and obsession with—the symbolism of right and left, mention of which is made in Appendix II of the present study. Of this design he observes that both Jehovah and Satan have their right feet forward, indicative of 'their spiritual correspondence with the earthly man who shows his left' (Wicksteed, p. 93). Cf. his Preface, pp. 14–15, and *passim*, and Appendix A. Fortunately or unfortunately the application of this discovery

cannot be made very happily in every case. Blake does allow right to have generally ameliorative and left to have generally pejorative value, but he is far from mechanical in his employment of such symbolism, and sometimes allows other considerations to have weight, as in Illustration XIX, where Job's left foot is forward in thoroughly hopeful and positive circumstances.

[3] Damon (p. 14) and Wicksteed (p. 95) both make this identification: Hagstrum (p. 132) tantalizingly proposes that the two heads represent Urizen and the Harlot of Babylon, but he gives no warrant for this suggestion.

[4] B & K 23.   [5] Hagstrum, p. 132.

[6] Wicksteed declares that the dog is a phallic symbol (Wicksteed, p. 96). I see no justification for this. Cf. my n. 4 to Illustration I.

two vine leaves resembling sheep's heads hanging from the serpent-creeper. Obviously the trees are portentous, for the single tree of Illustration I is divided, and division here as elsewhere indicates the fallen state.

There are many other portents in this Illustration. The incomplete arch of dark clouds in the design itself puts the drama depicted in the realm of outwardness rather than inwardness. Or rather the position of the clouds reinforces the theme delineated in the design, that of Job's outwardness. His *struggle*, however, is destined to be inward because he has neglected, he has refused to acknowledge, the things of the spirit. In the borders are mournful angels, regarding the smoke and fire issuing from entwined branches upon which perch insolently prideful peacocks and nesting birds—perhaps, as Damon suggests 'the parrot of vain repetitions'.[7] The reason for the mournfulness is that the smoke and fire are doubtless 'the pillars of cloud and flame that led the Israelites through the wilderness to Mount Sinai, where the Ten Commandments were revealed'—as Damon points out.[8]

What he does not say (perhaps he regards it as unnecessary to do so) is that Blake despised the negative commandments of the lawgivers and preferred the inner weather of the individual imagination.[9] That these representations are all contained within a gothically criss-crossed series of branches is, however, indicative of a less than ruinous eventual issue. But the fence in the lower border is incomplete: the central section is removed and the presence of the bull and the ram in the same relationship as in Illustration I, together with a somnolent dog, are signs of disorder. For while it is true that Job sees much, he sees falsely because singly. 'I shall see God' is prophecy. These words, engraved in the upper border, must be set beside 'We shall awake up in thy Likeness', the words from the seventeenth Psalm which have an ironic force here, but which on further examination point to a kind of vision which Job will one day acquire. Already Blake has wrenched the story away from Satan and put it where he thinks it belongs, in the darkening imagination of Job himself.

---

[7] Dict. 218.

[8] Damon, p. 14. Wicksteed believes the origin of the significance of the pillars of fire and cloud are probably to be found in

Blake's depictions of Luvah and his female counterpart Vala (Wicksteed, p. 97).

[9] See *The Everlasting Gospel*, E 510-16, K 748-59.

III. THE DESTRUCTION OF JOB'S SONS
overleaf

The Fire of God is

And the Lord said unto Satan Behold All that he hath is in thy Power

Fallen from Heaven

Thy Sons & thy Daughters were eating & drinking Wine in their
eldest Brothers house & behold there came a great wind from the Wilderness
& smote upon the four faces of the house & it fell upon the young Men & they are Dead

WBlake inven: & sculp

London, Published as the Act directs March 8: 1825 by Willm Blake N.º 3 Fountain Court Strand

III The Destruction of Job's Sons

In the Bible Job's sons are destroyed as a satanic challenge of faith. The challenge is from without. In the Blake narrative the destruction comes about because Job takes pride in the outward and visible signs of what he supposes to be an inward and spiritual grace. But the fact is that Job has shifted his allegiance from the inner to the outer life, and in order that he be brought to true spirituality he must be re-educated. He must witness the disintegration depicted here in his mind's eye, for the account of the destruction comes to him in the form of a report. And he must learn to endure the terrible news.

The design is dominated by a bat-winged Satan, presiding over the holocaust, and obviously its chief instrument. In Illustration II he had been vigorous and even graceful. Now he is vigorous still, but diminished in physique: more solid, perhaps older, and mindless in his blank-faced delight in causing havoc and destruction: a nightmare version of the son beneath him.[1] The bat-wings are extended, and he is partly squatting because one foot is pushing over a flat stone—an altar or column—and his other foot another. The architecture is Roman and therefore in Blake's view unfavourable. At the same time each hand grasps a piece of flame.

Below, among the ruins, are fifteen discernible figures. The central representation is the eldest son, holding an infant on his left shoulder, with suppliant members of his family at his feet. They want to be saved from destruction, all but two of them who are obviously already dead. One is a female stretched full length at the bottom of the design, her feet resting on a timbrel, and her left hand on a lyre. Such is the degradation and death of art. The other figure is a brother hanging by his feet upside down from the top of the steps, overturned vessels—material wealth destroyed—beside his head. This brother, behind whom appears to be another figure reduplicated, has his arms extended as in crucifixion. His expression is melancholy and resigned: is he the counterpart here to the Satan depicted, also arms extended, at the top of the design? In any event, as Wicksteed points out, the brother figure summons up Blake's bitter criticism of the Church.[2] 'The Modern Church', according to *A Vision of the Last Judgment*, 'Crucifies Christ with the Head Downwards',[3] and the steps behind the brother are perhaps an incipient cross.[4]

Whether all the figures depicted among the ruins are sons and their concubines is less important than the straightforward fact that Job's sons are here shown to be in the process of being destroyed. Job's family itself is in ruins. And Job's horrified imagination now faces up to the inescapable bad news. Job's own view, and the Illustration may be seen as his view, contains the partly-repressed reasons for the destruction. Job has neglected art[5] and eschewed sexual pleasure—he has denied joy itself—and all these are shown to be overthrown here by the Satan of his mind's eye. He has also attached a significance to family life which has been ruinous. 'Soft Family-Love' is bad because it excludes all the world beside and because it does not allow for individual differences:[6] familial duties can be destructive of the entire family unless enlivened and mollified by art.

---

[1] Anatomical counterpart and correspondence are deftly worked out here. Wicksteed observes, for instance, that Satan's right foot is advanced more than his left, although the left leg is before the right. This 'defiance of anatomical possibility' serves to illustrate the correspondence with the son beneath him, who also has the left foot forward.

[2] Wicksteed, p. 106. [3] E 554, K 615.

[4] Although it is impossible to be confident about the presence of the cross in this Illustration, identification is less uncertain in Illustrations VII and X. The cross was for Blake, as for Christians, a symbol of redemption. At the end of 1805 he wrote to William Hayley, a fellow artist as well as a patron: 'The mocker of Art is the Mocker of Jesus. Let us go on, Dear Sir, following his Cross: let us take it up daily, persisting in Spiritual Labours & the Use of that Talent which it is Death to Bury, & of that Spirit to which we are called.' (Letters, pp. 121–2, K 863.) It is in this positive way that the cross should, in my opinion, be seen in the Job designs.

[5] This point has been made by Hagstrum, p. 132.

[6] *Jerusalem*, Pl. 27. 77 (E 172, K 651). Wicksteed makes the first but not the second point about the family (p. 100), and in this respect attributes to Blake, correctly as it seems to me, what may be called a Chekhovian view of the possible selfishness of familial relationships. And Blake, in his latter days at least, was even more radical, as *The Everlasting Gospel* makes abundantly clear. In the design under consideration the muted musical instruments and the thwarted sexuality point to this more extreme view. Damon declares: 'The dissipation of the children can be ignored only so far. Job learns that his six younger sons have followed their eldest brother's example; they have all taken mistresses. Job's wrath explodes.' (Damon, p. 16.) Support for such a view can be found in the Biblical version (Job 1:4, 5, 13, 18, 19), but my own interpretation is closer to Blake's declared views in *Jerusalem* and *The Everlasting Gospel*.

The words written in a quarter-circle in the border above the design are, 'And the Lord said unto Satan Behold All that he hath is in thy Power' —the remainder of the sentence, not engraved by Blake, is, 'only upon himself put not forth thine hand.' But this Illustration does more than depict the limits set by God, at first, upon satanic power: it depicts that first stage itself, the design here being supported by the other words in the borders and by flames, smoke, and scaly creatures: scorpions or locusts and the tails of serpents.[7]

---

[7] Damon asserts that the border designs represent 'the great serpent, who is the religion Materialism' (Damon, p. 16). Such an interpretation is, in my view, too literal.

14

IV. THE MESSENGERS TELL JOB OF THE MISFORTUNES THAT HAVE
BEFALLEN HIM

overleaf

4

And there came a Messenger unto Job & said. The Oxen were plowing & the Sabeans came down. & they have slain the Young Men with the Sword

Going to & fro in the Earth

& walking up & down in it

And I only am escaped alone to tell thee.

While he was yet speaking
there came also another & said

The fire of God is fallen from heaven & hath burned up the flocks & the
Young Men & consumed them. & I only am escaped alone to tell thee

W Blake invent & sculp

London, Published as the Act directs March 8: 1825. by Will‎ᵐ Blake N°3 Fountain Court Strand.

IV The Messengers tell Job of the Misfortunes that have Befallen him

Chronologically, so far as the Bible story goes, this Illustration should precede III, since its subject is a report of the disasters that are depicted there. But in Blake's retelling of the story, the ordering is the more poignant because the more ironic: here Job and his wife still inhabit a stable world, although it is full of dark portent. They are sitting on a Druid seat beneath their no longer central tree, palms together piously, with but three sheep present. Behind them are two Druidic stone columns.[1] In this design all is still except the messengers, and so their frenzy is emphasized. The first messenger is so much in motion that his hair is flying behind him as he gives the news of the destruction by fire of the flocks and the servants. Behind him is another messenger carrying a shepherd's crook or cane. Behind him is a church, undoubtedly Gothic, even more recessive and shadowed than the church of Illustration I. There is a third running messenger dimly discernible on the hilltop.[2]

In the lower border lightning strikes. There is also fire, serpentine in form, which extends part way up the side borders, at the top of which clouds issue upward into the top border. On the right and left corners of a narrow blank margin between the design and the border proper lie two ineffectual spirits, one on each corner, heads and arms hanging down into the vertical borders, utterly incapable of providing, in their posture, either solace or hope. But the centre of attention in the top border is Satan, bat-winged and holding a sword and shield, standing with his back to the front of the Illustration, the very exemplar of the Law:

> When Satan first the black bow bent
> And the Moral Law from the Gospel rent
> He forged the Law into a Sword
> And spilld the blood of mercy s Lord.[3]

So Blake writes in the prefatory section to Chapter 3 of *Jerusalem*, a section addressed 'To the Deists'. In point of fact Job has been in the position of a Deist of the sort Blake describes in plain prose in the same preface: 'Your Religion, O Deists: Deism, is the Worship of the God of this World by the means of what you call Natural Religion and Natural Philosophy, and of Natural Morality or Self-Righteousness, the Selfish Virtues of the Natural Heart.'[4] The connection between design and border is established by Job's gaze: he is looking directly at the inward-turning Satan. The news of the misfortunes that have befallen his family has brought Job to the point of acknowledging a satanic element in his own view of the world. But he is unable to establish the connection in such a way as to assess his own role in the disaster. This incapacity is to be made clear in the following Illustration where Job tries to redeem himself by the techniques of outward observance, by exercising 'the Selfish Virtues of the Natural Heart'.

The importance of the left-right symbolism can be observed here in the insistent placement of left feet forward—of Job, of his wife, of the two nearest messengers, and of the sheep: no doubt the ram's placement, leftward of Job, is a portent. Above all, however, the composition of this design shows the self-possession of Job and his wife. What Job has done is perfectly usual in psychological terms. He has faced the horrors as long as possible, and then he has repressed them. He has rearranged himself—outwardly (for outward arrangements are the best he can make). He has not yet been bedevilled into the radical self-examination that will cause him to set forth on the path to redemption.

---

[1] Damon thinks these columns to be crosses, 'which will not be broken until Illustration XIX', when Job is saved (Damon, p. 18).

[2] The Butts, Linnell, and New Zealand series do not show this third figure.

[3] *Jerusalem*, Pl. 52. 17-20 (E 200, K 683).   [4] E 199, K 682.

Did I not weep for him who was in trouble Was not my Soul afflicted for the Poor

Behold he is in thy hand; but save his Life

Then went Satan forth from the presence of the Lord
And it grieved him at his heart
Who maketh his Angels Spirits & his Ministers a Flaming Fire

W Blake inventor & sculp

London, Published as the Act directs March 8: 1825, by Will'm Blake N° 3 Fountain Court Strand

V   Satan going forth from the Presence of the Lord

That Blake's interpretation of the Job story is to bear a distinctly modern emphasis, the emphasis suggested by Elihu alone among the friends, is indicated by the design of this Illustration, and by one of the questions in the border: 'Did I not weep for him who was in trouble? Was not my Soul afflicted for the Poor?' Blake has moved boldly many chapters ahead in the Job story to make the point that it is Job's own self-reliance—his illusion of self-sufficiency—that necessitates his trial.

Job and his wife sit sadly on a Druidic bench or altar. Job is giving half a loaf with his left hand to a poor man leaning upon his shepherd's crook, with an emaciated lamb or lamb-like dog on a lead. It is a material rather than a spiritual gesture, as the left hand indicates. As Job does not yet realize, mere giving is not tantamount to genuine piety: what makes for true godliness is the establishment of a relationship such that real reciprocity will take place—as it does in Illustration XIX, where Job will be seen to accept charity himself. For Blake the Kingdom of Heaven is on earth or it is nowhere. 'I am not God afar off,' Jesus declares in *Jerusalem*, 'I am a brother and a friend.'[1] Real spirituality centres on an inner awareness that manifests itself not in such a patronizing gesture as the half-loaf proffered with the left hand but in substantial deeds of men among men.

Behind Job and his wife and to their right on a slight rise is a Druidic altar which replaces the Gothic church of the previous Illustration. The sky is lighter. And, perhaps more remarkable in view of the fact that Job's severest trials are yet to come, two guardian angels hover at the lower edges of the design: Job is never to be abandoned—he is always to be watched over.

But the whole of the upper part of the design contains a circular inset framed by flames and connected to Job in that all focus on the phial held by Satan next to Job's right ear. Once more the upper part of the design is given over to what is going on in the mind of Job. The impression is strengthened by the contrapuntal appearance and position of Job's god in the design. Two stones make the base of his seat, and he holds a closed book in his right hand, a scroll in his left—the counterparts to Job's half-loaves, emblems of outwardness. His uneasiness of posture reflects Job's own spiritual disquiet.

Satan's bat-wings are gone, and, instead of looking full of the lust of destruction as he does in Illustration III, he shares the general anxiety; he holds his left arm up, as if to ward off a blow. The reason for this alteration in countenance is that Satan, despite the phial of spiritual poison, is perhaps less confident than formerly of his capacity to subvert Job. Since this vision is Job's own, the significance is that the patriarch has emerged from the stages of self-righteousness (this was blasted by the terrible destruction visited upon him) and apathy: he is now endeavouring, however inadequately, to bestir himself; and satanic power becomes, though ever so slightly, contained.

None the less, God—who has now granted new powers to Satan—looks too mournful and passive and old to deal with this young and powerful Satan; and the twelve angelic figures nearest Satan are floating fearfully away from him, swathed like Satan himself in fiery winds. The principal text, set immediately beneath the framed design itself, is, 'Then went Satan forth from the presence of the Lord', but the remaining texts, which make a coherent sentence when put together with the opening phrase from Job, are from Genesis and Psalms respectively. In Blake's conflation there is the depiction of a Jehovah of sacrifice, a diabolical figure. The scaly serpents and flames and palms in the borders support this theme. There is also, however, a grieving but no longer supine and thus no longer impotent angel on each of the upper corners.

---

[1] *Jerusalem*, Pl. 4. 18 (E 145, K 622).

6

Naked came I out of my mothers womb & Naked shall I return thither
The Lord gave & the Lord hath taken away. Blessed be the Name of the Lord

And smote Job with sore Boils
from the sole of his foot to the crown of his head

W Blake inv & sc.

London, as Act directs Published March 8: 1825 by William Blake N 3 Fountain Court Strand.

VI Satan smiting Job with Boils

This Illustration depicts a grievously tortured Job, but the very physical manifestations point to something more fundamental: shame. In *Jerusalem* the hero Albion in a distinctly parallel situation cries out:

The disease of Shame covers me from head to feet. I have no hope.
Every boil upon my body is a separate & deadly Sin.
Doubt first assaild me, then Shame took possession of me.[1]

Satan is depicted here as a strong, vigorous, and even graceful youth. He stands with joyful triumph on an anguished Job. Satan's arms are extended in the cruciform position, and a halo is formed behind his head: Job's god has become devilish, and this is the most painful fact of all. In Satan's left hand is the phial with which he is smiting Job with sore boils; the fiery liquid of spiritual anguish is being poured upon the naked patriarch. Behind Satan's right hand are four flaming arrows, unquestionably the arrows of the Almighty later referred to by Job in reply to the comfort of Eliphaz:[2] 'The arrows of the Almighty are within me, the poison whereof drinketh up my spirit: the terrors of God do set themselves in array against me.'[3]

Lying on a bed of what appear to be palm fronds, Job is partly raised up in the anguish which Satan is visiting upon him. He wears the sack-cloth of which the Biblical Job speaks.[4] His head is flung back, his eyes are open and staring backward, away from the approaching fire from the phial. His hands are lifted, perhaps partly in supplication, against the agony. His feet rest upon the knees of a grieving wife, who is no longer at his side for she is beyond being able to bring comfort to her husband. Druidic ruins[5] strew the landscape in the middle ground and background of the design, and the sun sets beyond black water.[6] In the sky the black and billowing clouds all centre on Satan; they look to be the clouds of fire that are being funnelled through Satan's phial.

In the borders are horrid shapes. The angels in the upper corners of the blank margins are standing or floating with languid or blank aspects, and each has now grown a bat-wing. Each, furthermore, holds a poisonous spider, depending from a long strand of web. Two other bat-winged angels appear in the upper border, evidently within a rift in the billowing cloud that floats there. In the lower border are a couple of steps leading nowhere, a broken shepherd's crook, a grasshopper,[7] and—in the centre—an earthenware pot from which a fragment has been broken, doubtless the potsherd used by Job to scrape himself with in his agony, to relieve the pain of the boils.[8] On the right is a frog, the fragment of the pot, palm leaves ('of suffering'),[9] ilex leaves, and three thistles, spoken of despairingly by Job in the Bible story.[10] These disordered and pejorative symbols frame Job's spiritual torture. Their clarity and distinctness of outline, however, manifest their inescapably substantive existence. Within the design itself the recessive and scaled-over genitalia[11] betray the terrible triumph of diseased will over spiritual—and thus necessarily physical—well-being.

---

[1] *Jerusalem*, Pl. 21. 3–5 (E 164, K 643).

[2] My interpretation of the significance of the arrows differs from but does not contradict that of Damon, who declares that they indicate 'the death of four of Job's senses', but since the four arrows are adverted to in the Biblical version itself (6:4) I believe that my narrower view is the more likely. Cf. Damon, p. 22.

[3] Job 6:4.

[4] Job 16:15.

[5] Wicksteed speaks of 'the patriarchal courts . . . ruined and deserted' (Wicksteed, p. 121). This is a fine speculation.

[6] Wicksteed believes the setting sun to be emblematic of Job's wife's despairing soul (Wicksteed, p. 126).

[7] See, for instance, *Milton*, Pl. 27. 13–19 (E 123, K 513), where the grasshopper (see below) also appears. Bildad in the Bible story speaks of trust 'of all that forget God' as 'a spider's web' (Job 8:13–14).

[8] Job 2:8.

[9] *Jerusalem*, Pl. 59. 6 (E 206, K 691).

[10] Job 31:40. And Blake writes twice, each time in almost identical language, of the thistle's malevolence. In *Vala* the following lines appear:

The indignant Thistle whose bitterness is bred in his milk,
And who lives on the contempt of his neighbour.
(Night IX, E 389, K 377; cf. *Milton*, Pl. 27. 26, E 123, K 513.)

Damon points out that some of these symbols appear in the last chapter of Ecclesiastes, where the preacher warns of the day when 'the grasshopper shall be a burden, and desire shall fail . . . the pitcher be broken at the fountain . . . the wheel broken at the cistern' (Eccles. 12:5). Cf. Dict. 219. But Damon reads the fifth verse in such a way as to make the grasshopper symbolic of dying desire. The point, however, of these ugly and desiccated border symbols is unambiguous.

[11] Damon argues that the boils and encrusted genitalia together indicate Job's sense of sexual guilt, and he is surely right in making the connection, boils being 'traditionally the signs of a venereal disease', but sexual disease and derangement are emblematic of a more general disorder. Cf. Damon, p. 22.

7

What! shall we recieve Good
at the hand of God & shall we not also
recieve Evil

And when they lifted up their eyes afar off & knew him not
they lifted up their voice & wept, & they rent every Man his
mantle & sprinkled dust upon their heads towards heaven

Ye have heard of the Patience of Job and have seen the end of the Lord.

W Blake inven & sculpt

London. Published as the Act directs March 8. 1825 by William Blake N3 Fountain Court Strand

VII   Job's Comforters

'Corporeal friends', as Blake had reason to know at first hand, 'are spiritual enemies': so this well-known line from both *Milton* and *Jerusalem* insists,[1] and the reason, in the Job series, is clearly set forth. The friends, with their 'insulting benevolences', bring the cold comforts of reproof. Like Blake's sometime patron the poetaster William Hayley, Job's corporeal friends feel themselves entitled to sit in judgement—but such a posture is godlike in its assumption of superiority. It is also stupid in its supposition that Job is like themselves. Thus in Blake's lexicon 'corporeal' is privative: friendship involves a spiritual communion realized in the flesh; when the spirituality is absent, when the relationship is one of mere corporeality, friendship is necessarily false.

Job himself is seated as if exhausted on a little mound of hay or straw, his hands palm downward, his face in the attitude of pained resignation that naturally follows upon his severe trials. His head, which reposes on the breast of his wife, who kneels behind him, supporting him, looks toward his left and upward to what appears to be a cross. Although it is incipient (the crosspiece being very little longer than the width of the vertical piece), its position at the edge of the design commands attention, for it is what Job looks toward. Job's wife, whose face is racked with distress, looks not at the cross but at her husband; and the pain on her face appears to be at once more acute and less profound than that of Job himself, who for all the grief mirrored in his features is able to sustain himself the more adequately.

The motif of the cross is repeated in the lower right-hand corner of the design, so that the right side of the Illustration is dominated top and bottom by the emblem of redemption. This motif is the more strongly emphasized by the contrast formed with what is evidently a Druid altar, and with a number of Druidic ruins in the middle ground and background. At the rear of the design is a pair of black hills, suggestive of female breasts and therefore distinctly apposite here, for the words engraved in the upper border are the pious and defensive question uttered by Job in response to his wife's entreaty, 'Curse God, and die'.

Sorrow is the theme of the border designs. In the lower border a shepherdess, leaning against a leafless tree, looks groundward, her crook in her left hand; a dog looks expectantly up at her.[2] Across the lower border is depicted a featureless stretch of land, with a single clump of trees, the analogue to the cross in the design. On the other side of the lower border, and also leaning against a leafless tree, is an old shepherd, with sheep and a ram lying down at his feet. These human figures bear strong resemblances to Job and his wife. They thus reduplicate and universalize the sorrow of the hero of the narrative. Written across the face of the desert or plain are the words of the Fourth Gospel: 'Ye have heard of the Patience of Job and have seen the end of the Lord.' And it is true that already, in the design itself, Job does wear a patient aspect. The sorrowing angels on either corner of the top border are no doubt weeping for Job, and their tears are ultimately suggestive of hope: at the beginning of the story the hero was too self-sufficient to be capable of learning from experience. Before the jolts of disaster overthrew him he was like his three friends, secure, as he thought, in the knowledge of what life signified, and of his place in the universe, such that he might offer outward propitiation for the presumed sins of his sons. Now he has been dislocated into a realization of the pride, the precariousness, the opacity of his position. Though much suffering lies ahead of him he is embarked on the journey that will bring him to a chastened and literally transfigured sense of self.

---

[1] *Milton*, Pl. 4. 26 (E 97, K 484); *Jerusalem*, Pl. 44. 10 (E 191, K 655).

[2] Hagstrum says that the two figures here are 'an old and a young shepherd', but the figure on the left is surely female. Cf.

Hagstrum, p. 133. Damon identifies the figures in the margin as Job and his wife, 'still shepherds of Innocence, enduring their sorrows of Experience with resignation' (Damon, p. 24).

8

Lo let that night be solitary
& let no joyful voice come therein

Let the Day perish wherein I was Born

And they sat down with him upon the ground seven days & seven
nights & none spake a word unto him for they saw that his grief
was very great

W Blake inv & sculp

London. Publish'd as the Act directs March 8: 1825 by Will.m Blake N.o 3 Fountain Court Strand

VIII Job's Despair

Roused from his torpor, and perhaps inspired by his glimpse of the cross in Illustration VII, Job is here at the centre of the design, still seated to be sure, but with arms flung above his head, palms extended, and fingers open and separated: he looks not so much up as forward; his very tears are effulgent. His mouth is open, and he is unquestionably roaring out the words which are engraved in the lower and upper borders. There is nobility in his face, for his cries of despair proceed from a position of faith: neither in the Bible nor in Blake's narrative does Job deny God; he is never tempted to succumb to unbelief.[1]

Job's isolation—for isolation is one of the necessary conditions of despair—is emphasized by the fact that his face alone is depicted. His wife's face is concealed by her streaming hair, as are the faces of the friends.[2] Their relationship to the truth is suggested by the presence of a Druid pile behind them—with, as if for emphasis, a Romanesque arch.[3]

In the background are two hills or mountains,[4] no doubt the same ones depicted in Illustration VII, but here the hill on Job's right is askew, and behind it rise pillars of cloud, the upward thrust of which suggests an analogue in nature to Job's own posture, and they, like Job's despair, will disappear as the Little Black Boy of the lyric teaches:

And these black bodies and this sun-burnt face
Is but a cloud, and like a shady grove.
For when our souls have learn'd the heat to bear
The cloud will vanish we shall hear his voice.[5]

In the lower border is vegetation to match: an uprooted tropical tree; with withered fruit hanging from its overtaxed and deadened branches, and, across the bottom of the lower border, twisted in the shape of a serpent, the branch of a briar. In the middle of the lower border a couple of toadstools grow, each at an angle, repeating the tilt of the hill; and behind them in the background, two clumps of what appear to be desiccated thistles. In the lower right-hand border is a cactus or thistle, and there are drooping branches, balancing those of the lower left border. All these are outward and visible signs of Job's spiritual dryness—except for the small but numerous raindrops and blossoms, the counterpart of Job's tears.

The theme of this Illustration is expressed well in *Jerusalem*, where a lamenting spectre puts his own case for despair:

Prayer is vain. I called for compassion: compassion
   mock d;
Mercy & pity threw the grave stone over me & with lead
and iron bound it over me for ever, Life lives on my
Consuming: & the Almighty hath made me his Contrary
To be all evil, all reversed & for ever dead: knowing
And seeing life, yet living not; how can I then behold
And not tremble? how can I be beheld & not abhorr d?[6]

---

[1] Wicksteed declares that Job's slightly advanced left foot indicates his increasing despair (Wicksteed, p. 133).

[2] Compare *The Complaint of Job*, a water-colour drawing in sepia reproduced as Pl. 70 in *William Blake's Illustrations to the Bible*. In the water-colour Job's face looks more indignant and less harrowed than in the engraved design. Again, in the water-colour Job's arms are hanging down by his side, palms open. Finally in the water-colour the faces of Job's wife and of the three friends are visible, rather than abjectly hidden as in the engraving. The impression given by the water-colour is softer than that produced by the engraving.

[3] Damon sees a cross above the friends. I do not. Cf. Damon, p. 26.

[4] Wicksteed argues that they symbolize ' "demonstrative truth" which for Blake meant materialism' (Wicksteed, p. 134). The allusion is to the mountains that appear at the beginning of *Jerusalem*. There the hero, the fallen Albion, rejects the pleas of the Holy One and insists on outwardness, materiality, self-hood.

By demonstration man alone can live, and not by faith.
My mountains are my own, and I will keep them to myself.
                    (*Jerusalem*, Pl. 4. 28-9, E 145, K 622.)

Here, however, I prefer an interpretation that carries on the pejorative female symbolism of Illustration VII.

[5] E 9, K 125.

[6] *Jerusalem*, Pl. 10. 51-9 (E 152, K 630).

9

Shall mortal Man be more Just than God? Shall a Man be more Pure than his Maker? Behold he putteth no trust in his Saints & his Angels he chargeth with folly

W Blake invent & sculp

Then a Spirit passed before my face
the hair of my flesh stood up

London, Published as the Act directs March 8: 1825 by William Blake N 3 Fountain Court Strand

IX   The Vision of Eliphaz

The stern solace of Eliphaz the Temanite is the subject of this Illustration. Job and his wife, both of them seated on the ground, are looking upward at the scene envisioned for them—or at least for Job—by Eliphaz, who looks coldly toward them,[1] his left arm raised to its full height, indicating the scene referred to in the words engraved in the lower border. Behind Eliphaz are the two other friends, kneeling in attitudes of terrified piety.

The scene which forms the central point of Eliphaz's story is set by the teller himself, lying down for the night, his eyes distended by the vision before him: God, tall, imposing, haloed, gazes at him grimly. Eliphaz's words, engraved in the upper border, point to one of the rebukes he lays upon Job, namely that Job is guilty of the blasphemy of putting himself above God.[2] Of central importance here is the resemblance between the Eliphaz who is rebuking Job and the God who is depicted in the design, for Job begins to see, in the identification of Eliphaz with God, the nature of his own blasphemy. The impact is so powerful that Job has a deeply stricken look—and, again clearly from his own viewpoint, his wife is diminished and weakened in appearance. Job has been wrong to think himself a god, but Eliphaz is wrong to imagine the separability of the divine and the human; his theology of hierarchal remoteness leads paradoxically to the same patronizing posture from which Job has been dislodged.

The borders contain no figures of any kind, human or celestial; and the blasted, leafless trees, with drooping and probably broken branches, that appear on either side of the borders, give sting to the aridness of the words of Eliphaz. The cloud formation of the borders is deflated and unpromising.

---

[1] Wicksteed considers it significant here that Eliphaz's left side only is shown, while his God is shown with his right side foremost (Wicksteed, p. 135).

[2] This God is, as Damon points out, Pahad, the terrifying fifth eye (Damon, p. 28). Cf. Dict. 316. Wicksteed believes that Eliphaz's dream marks the beginning of Job's salvation, this being indicated by the fact that Job's right hand and arm are partially raised (Wicksteed, p. 135).

10

But he knoweth the way that I take
when he hath tried me I shall come forth like gold

Have pity upon me! Have pity upon me! O ye my friends
for the hand of God hath touched me

Though he slay me yet will I trust in him

The Just Upright Man is laughed to scorn

Man that is born of a Woman is of few days & full of trouble
he cometh up like a flower & is cut down, he fleeth also as a shadow
& continueth not. And dost thou open thine eyes upon such a one
& bringest me into judgment with thee

W Blake invent & sculp

London, Published as the Act directs March 8: 1825. by William Blake N3 Fountain Court Strand

X Job rebuked by his Friends

A tearful Job asks for pity; one of the texts in the upper border says as much. But his countenance, his posture, his physique are forceful because he has faith: 'Though he slay me yet will I trust in him.' These words, after the satanic trial depicted in Illustration VI, are of splendid directness. Indeed the effect of the design as a whole is painfully immediate: the three friends, now Job's harsh accusers, are seated on his left, their arms outstretched and fingers pointing at him.[1] His wife, significantly, is not kneeling; despite her tears she is isolated by incomprehension: she looks attentive, as though she will acknowledge the force of their accusations. She is in a state of despair less remediable because her faith is more superficial than Job's. Her tears are those of self-pity, for she thinks the friends may be right.

The expressions on the faces of the accusers are self-righteous, and they are looking not so much at as toward Job: their hearts are so hardened that they cannot see. They cannot pity. Their relationship to the patriarch is articulated in the lower border, containing a sentence from the chapter in which Job, having rejected the comfort of his friends, turns on Zophar and in effect scorns the judgement of one mortal upon another. Job himself has much to learn but the trials he has undergone have taught him the important truth that sympathy rather than judgement is what is required among men.

In this design Job is being driven from his hopes for human sympathy to a confrontation with the God who has caused him, as he thinks, to despair. His communication with his friends is directed to the end of self-justification, but he finds himself able to make a plain challenge that justifies the massive cross-like capital which rises above his wife in the design. The trio of mottoes in the upper border, enclosed in an incomplete Roman arch and taken from three considerably separated chapters of the Book of Job, point to this shift.

The border decorations are bleak. The two angels on the upper corners appear to be holding with difficulty to the flat upper border of the blank margin between the design and the border. They are being pulled downward, or at least weighed down, by chains. Bat-wings protrude from the lower corners of the margin; and in the lower border 'the cuckoo of slander,[2] the owl of false wisdom,[3] and the adder of hate . . . mock the scrolls of true inspiration'. None the less the effect of the whole is positive. Job's adherence to his faith grants him a heroic stature that dominates and redeems the accusation and the despair of the Illustration. The small flower[4] beneath the hands of the accusers, the recessive Druidic stones behind them, and the lightening sky behind the hills, give a substantial hope that the promise held out by the cross will be fulfilled.

---

[1] In the drawing at the Tate Gallery (Blake Catalogue 5200) in which this scene is represented, the three friends look very much more sorrowful—less accusing, more friendly. (Two versions of this design, one more highly finished than the other, can be found in Keynes's *Blake Studies*, Pls. 31 and 32.) Furthermore the separate engravings of this subject show a self-righteous Job and extremely accusing friends, but the accusations are mainly from their baleful eyes: their arms are not extended as in Illustration X here. See Keynes's *Engravings by William Blake* (Dublin, 1956), where these engravings are reproduced as Pls. 6

and 7. All in all the engraving for the Job series of 1826 is superior to its predecessors.

[2] Damon, p. 30. Damon goes on to say, less credibly, that the scrolls are by way of being a reply to Blake's critics 'who attacked his work so blindly and unmercifully'.

[3]   The Owl that calls upon the Night
         Speaks the Unbelievers fright
                ('Auguries of Innocence', E 482, K 431.)

[4] Wicksteed interprets the flower as the symbol of man's frailty and temporality (Wicksteed, p. 137).

11

My bones are pierced in me in the night season & my sinews take no rest

My skin is black upon me & my bones are burned with heat

The triumphing of the wicked is short, the joy of the hypocrite is but for a moment
Satan himself is transformed into an Angel of Light & his Ministers into Ministers of Righteousness

With Dreams upon my bed thou scarest me & affrightest me with Visions

Why do you persecute me as God & are not satisfied with my flesh, Oh that my words were printed in a Book that they were graven with an iron pen & lead in the rock for ever For I know that my Redeemer liveth & that he shall stand in the latter days upon the Earth & after my skin destroy thou This body yet in my flesh shall I see God whom I shall see for Myself and mine eyes shall behold & not Another tho consumed be my wrought Image Who opposeth & exalteth himself above all that is called God or is Worshipped

W Blake invent & sculp

London, Published as the Act directs March 8: 1825 by Will Blake N 3 Fountain Court Strand

XI Job's Evil Dreams

The extreme agony which Job is seen to be suffering in this design stems from friendly comfort, but is exacerbated by self-knowledge and terrible isolation. The central text is contained in a chapter given over to Job's reply to Eliphaz's rebukes: 'With Dreams upon my bed thou scarest me & affrightest me with Visions.' For the agony depicted in the design is precisely that of Job dreaming with his eyes open. His body licked by flames[1] both below him and on the far side of his bed, Job is lying on his back, his hands pushing away from him the immense and cloven-footed God–Satan, whose leg and hoof are entwined by a scaly serpent.[2] The satanic countenance is the counterpart of Job's face, and Job now recognizes the terrifying fact that in making God in his own image he has created the selfhood that is Satan.[3] This is the reason why the visions frighten him more than anything else has done.

Job's legs and thighs are gripped from beneath by the clawed fingers of two scaly demons, while a third approaches in the sea of flames, clutching the chain of moral law[4] with which he evidently means to torture or bind Job. These demons replace the friends of the previous Illustration,[5] the accusers whose strictures are now seen for what they are: demonic.

Issuing from the back of the satanic hoof is a streak of dark lightning that runs across the top of the design. The sky is dark, and there is a pair of arched stones on which Hebrew lettering can be discerned: these are tablets of religious law and the God–Satan points to them with his right hand. For Job has lived by the law, by the letter, and to live by outward observance is to misconstrue tragically the nature of God's injunctions, though Job does not yet know this.

All the texts in the borders articulate the tortures illustrated in the design. But the lower border contains the still unshaken assertion of faith—'I know that my redeemer liveth.' Blake's preoccupation with the subject-matter of this centrally important Illustration is reflected in the similarities to be found in the colour print at the Tate Gallery of *Elohim Creating Adam* (1795, Blake Catalogue 5055), in that the Elohim and Adam are in very much the same positions as the Satan–God and Job of the Illustration. While it would be a mistake to press a comparison between the present Illustration and the colour print, there is something to be gained by observing that the Elohim and Adam are notably dissimilar, whereas Job and his god are identical: Job, still imprisoned in his selfhood, is tortured in part at least because he cannot see beyond himself.[6] Blake's alteration of the King James translation substantiates this fact. Blake alters 'after my skin worms destroy this body' to 'after my skin destroy thou this body'.[7] The shift indicates Job's presumption. The alteration of another phrase here is equally significant. Blake changes 'though my reins be consumed within me' to 'tho consumed be my wrought Image': Job still imagines that conformance with the letter—if only the letter can be known—will suffice, but such is conformance with the law of the god of this world. In fact Satan is triumphing here, but—as Jenijoy LaBelle points out in an unpublished paper—'his triumph will end when Job recognizes his error. The very words "my wrought Image" are already starting to go up in flames in the lower right hand corner of the border.' Pictorially the theme of this Illustration is substantiated by the jaggedness of the design. In all the previous Illustrations there is a roundedness which here gives way to the starkness of Job's nadir.

---

[1] Wicksteed notes that while the movement of the flames in this Illustration is counter-clockwise, the movement of God–Satan and the serpent is clockwise—that is, redemptive; and he cites, by way of corroboration, the following Proverb of Hell: 'If the fool would persist in his folly he would become wise' (E 36, K 151) (Wicksteed, p. 148).

[2] 'the serpent of Materialism' (Damon, p. 32).

[3] This Satan is 'Worshipd as God by the Mighty Ones of the Earth' (*Jerusalem*, Pl. 29. 18 (E 173, K 659)). Cf. Wicksteed, p. 146.

[4] 'Blake hates the moral law, of which the chain is the symbol, yet he gives to it a regenerative function. . . . The fact that the chain has its inception in heaven and that the end must return

to the beginning, signifies that the law must conclude in its own annulment.' (Percival, pp. 61–2.)

[5] Wicksteed also points out that the demons replace the friends (Wicksteed, p. 145).

[6] There is an interesting parallel in the colour print *God Judging Adam*, also at the Tate Gallery (1795, Blake Catalogue 5063). Here God and Adam are virtually identical in physique and facial feature. This colour print and *Elohim Creating Adam* are both reproduced in colour in Martin Butlin, *William Blake* (London, 1966).

[7] Damon's interpretation is that the changes point to an emphasis by Blake on a meaning that 'the spiritual body survives the physical' (Damon, p. 32).

12

For God speaketh once yea twice & Man perceiveth it not

In a Dream in a Vision of the Night in deep Slumberings upon the bed Then he openeth the ears of Men & sealeth their instruction

That he may withdraw Man from his purpose & hide Pride from Man
If there be with him an Interpreter One among a Thousand

then he is gracious unto him & saith Deliver him from going down to the Pit I have found a Ransom

For his eyes are upon the ways of Man & he observeth all his goings

I am Young & ye are very Old wherefore I was afraid

Lo all these things worketh God oftentimes with Man to bring back his Soul from the pit to be enlightened with the light of the living

Look upon the heavens & behold the clouds which are higher than thou

If thou sinnest what doest thou against him. or if thou be righteous what givest thou unto him

WBlake inven it & sculpt

London Published as the Act directs March 8: 1825 by Will.m Blake N 3 Fountain Court Strand

XII   The Wrath of Elihu

Elihu's wrath is of a special kind, and it is of special importance to the Blake narrative.[1] Within the design itself all the human figures are motionless, except for Elihu himself, whose features are evidently working as he administers his reproaches to Job, and indeed to the three friends as well. 'I am Young', he says, '& ye [plural] are very Old.' Elihu's arms are raised in gesticulation: with his left hand he is pointing to the sky; his right arm is extended toward Job, and his palm is raised and open, as if in benediction. That is to say his wrath is not righteous indignation: it is an anger tempered by sympathy and by hope.

In this design attention is immediately arrested by the youth of Elihu: his figure is passionate, lucid, and eloquent. The three friends are squatting on their knees in front of a Druidic altar or pile: their faces bear the blank look of intransigence, for their ears are closed to the admonitions of the young man. Job too, sitting in the centre of the design, his arms folded across his chest, looks not at Elihu but straight ahead into the middle distance, evidently discomfited by the lessons which Elihu wants to teach him. But his wife—who in Illustration X stared back at the friends even though she appeared to be grief-struck—now sits, her head buried in her knees, her face wholly concealed, and her hands folded together penitently. At last even she may be able to accomplish regeneration. Above all the pictorial contrast between youth and age suggests not the finality of punishment but the hope of renewal this side of the grave.

Another commanding aspect of this Illustration is the twelve stars against the black night sky behind Elihu, who makes them a part of his lesson. These stars appear also, all twelve of them, in the upper border. They suggest the twelve sons of Israel, and here

they point to a return, the redemption envisioned in Revelation 7.[2] An apposite symbolic suggestion made by the stars is that of the relationship between man and God. Blake is specific on this point in *Vala*:

Thus were the stars of heaven created like a gold chain
To bind the Body of Man to heaven from falling into the
  Abyss.[3]

The single star, under the Druidic arch, indicates regeneration even under or despite the aegis of the religion of sacrifice.

Beneath Elihu's legs are a purse and two pieces of money.[4] Two possibly related explanations make sense: that Job has flung these to the ground in the realization that his charitable acts have been pietistic rather than the expression of an authentic $\chi\acute{\alpha}\rho\iota\varsigma$; that the purse and money are there to point forward to the moment when Job becomes not patron but beneficiary, a relationship depicted in Illustration XIX.

All the words engraved in the borders are those of Elihu himself. In the previous Illustration Job's slumbers have been troubled by horrid visions. In this Illustration a sleeping Job is shown lying in the lower border, but here the dreams are of the angelic figures engraved in the vertical and upper borders.[5] Job's left hand is upon a scroll—the word made flesh, the letter spiritualized. Stretched upon soft grass and pillowed on a thick tuft, Job is virtually surrounded by the spirits floating upward and forming finally an arch. In the background of the design are ruins, probably Druidic ruins, and behind them a single black hill or mountain peak along a range of dark hills. These are faint and recessive. For, in the words of Elihu engraved in the lower border, Job's soul is to be brought back 'from the pit to be enlightened with the light of the living'.

---

[1] The place of Elihu's speeches in the Biblical narrative is discussed exhaustively by E. Dhorme, *A Commentary on the Book of Job*, trans. Harold Knight (London, 1967), pp. xcviii–cx. Professor Dhorme's effort is to show the relevance of the speeches to the Job story, 'the resumption of a theme which had already been completed by the first author' (p. ciii). Northrop Frye considers Blake's Elihu to be making a summary of the arguments of the three friends: 'he is trying to consolidate their confused and variable notions of natural religion into a single closed system of fatalism.' ('Blake's Reading of the Book of Job', in Alvin H. Rosenfeld, ed., *William Blake: Essays for S. Foster Damon* (Providence, R.I., 1969), p. 227). But such an interpretation undervalues the visual joy of the design as a whole.

[2] Damon writes of Blake's use of the Sons of Israel. Cf. Dict. 201–2.

[3] E 315, K 287. The point is made by Wicksteed, who speculates—rather tentatively—that the stars 'may be the souls of other men, as distantly perceived by him [Job] across the abyss of nature, which in this corporeal life separates man from man' (Wicksteed, p. 155).

[4] B & K (p. 33) and Wicksteed (p. 157) believe this to be a broken potsherd—mistakenly, as it seems to me.

[5] Wicksteed discerns four streams of angelic figures, and speculates that each is identifiable in Blake's scheme of fourfold vision (Wicksteed, p. 156).

Who is this that darkeneth counsel by words without knowledge

Then the Lord answered Job out of the Whirlwind

Who maketh the Clouds his Chariot & walketh on the Wings of the Wind

the Drops of the Dew

Hath the Rain

a Father & who hath begotten

WBlake invenit & sculp

London Published as the Act directs March 8:1825 by William Blake N:3 Fountain Court Strand

XIII The Lord answering Job out of the Whirlwind

The answer from the whirlwind finds Job and his wife, more tender and gentle than formerly, close together. Behind them and barely discernible is a series of classical columns, certainly recessive.[1] Job and his wife are both looking toward God, whose appearance is tranquil,[2] even though the hair of his head and his beard swirl with the wind. There is in his eyes a compassionate expression, and his right hand is placed over Job's head, in a gesture of benediction. And just here a comparison should be made, to the water-colour called 'The Lord Answering Job Out of the Whirlwind, on Job Confessing His Presumption to God', reproduced as Plate 71 in *William Blake's Illustrations to the Bible*. In the water-colour the Lord and Job are not dissimilar in appearance, but Job's head and to some extent his beard are concealed beneath a cowl. In the engraving, however, the fact of identity is proclaimed in the shape and arrangement of hair and beard. Obviously Blake in the engraving wanted to underscore the resemblance of Job and the Lord, in order to demonstrate the transfiguration of Job himself.

The central and dominant position of God indicates the restoration of the relationship with Job. Job's wondrous response to the appearance of the Lord in the whirlwind occurs in part because Job acknowledges that he is in God's image, not contrariwise, as before. That this is a matter of central concern to Blake is indicated not only in a comparison between the earlier water-colours and the engraved Illustration but in the following lines that express the matter as well:

> He who sees the Infinite in all things sees God. He who sees the Ratio only sees himself only.
> Therefore God becomes as we are, that we may be as he is.[3]

In the lower border are three roots pulled almost entirely from the soil that nourishes them; and the texts engraved here, pointing to the divine creation of the rain, support the depiction of what is no doubt becoming re-rooted, the tree of life itself. In the upper border, the seven eyes are to be detected, agents of redemption pursuing their course in the circle of destiny.[4] This Illustration makes so signal a break not with the plot of the Biblical narrative but with its import that the reader must look astonished at the mildness, the humanity, and the tenderness even in this divine manifestation. In the Bible the Lord magisterially reminds Job of the inscrutability of divine purpose; in Blake's version awe gives way to the gentler shock of recognition. Only the friends, who have abased themselves in terror, fail to understand the import of what has happened.

---

[1] These are very clearly depicted, though still recessive, in the Butts water-colour; in the Linnell water-colour, there appear to be three columns. Wicksteed, somewhat puzzlingly, writes of 'the obscurely discernible balustrade behind Job and his wife. This represents the "motive" of the Gothic church and Druid altar in the earlier designs, and is expressive of Job's religion. Its effect in the first place is to reinforce the conception of Job's restored prosperity, by giving the impression of the scene being enacted upon the broad terrace of a lordly house. But there is a special significance in the form of balustrade. For unlike the pagan cairns and altars or even the Gothic church, it is something that carries the mind away beyond the design into a larger world, the world of which Job suddenly finds himself a part; a part though insignificantly small, still, in virtue of its perfect love, prince and possessor of the whole.' (Wicksteed, pp. 162-3.) Such an interpretation is resourceful and pertinacious but undemonstrable.

[2] Wicksteed makes much of the fact that the cloud belt is *above* God here, for the cloud belt 'always marks the bound between our earth and heaven', and thus God is not within but manifested in outward nature. For speculations on this point, see Wicksteed, pp. 160, 163-6. Cf. Appendix II to the present commentary.

[3] *There is no Natural Religion* (b) (E 2, K 98). The fact that the whirlwind (and also the border figures) moves in a clockwise direction is also indicative of the redemptive force of this design, as Wicksteed points out (Wicksteed, p. 160).

[4] This interpretation is simpler than that of Hagstrum, who says, 'The God of the design anticipates the new, but the God of the border is the old Urizen swirling about, in nature's eternal round, a classic and Druidic arch.' (Hagstrum, p. 134.) This is perhaps excessively elaborate, but Wicksteed's is even more so. He writes of 'the figure of the patriarch in the margin endlessly imaged as links of the chain that repeats the conception of great Nature's diurnal round. For when once the Self is laid to sleep in man, as we have seen it laid to sleep in the previous margin, it wakes again in infinite multitude, becoming the key and interpretation of the abounding life of the Universe.' (Wicksteed, p. 161.) In the water-colour reproduced as Plate 71 in *William Blake's Illustrations to the Bible* there are but six figures, winged and beardless. In the Illustration Blake as usual makes himself clearer. None the less, Damon counts but six Eyes (Damon, p. 36).

14

Canst thou bind the sweet influences of Pleiades or loose the bands of Orion

Let there Be

Light

Let there be A

Firmament

Let the Waters be gathered together into one place

& let the Dry Land appear

And God made Two Great Lights

Sun

Moon

Let the Waters bring forth abundantly

Let the Earth bring forth

Cattle & Creeping thing & Beast

When the morning Stars sang together, & all the
Sons of God shouted for joy

W Blake Inventit & Sc

London. Published as the Act directs March 8. 1825 by Will Blake N 3 Fountain Court Strand.

XIV   The Creation

Supported by texts not only from Job but also from Genesis, this design and its borders depict the creation. A question which immediately asks itself is why Blake puts the beginning so late, exactly two-thirds of the way through his narrative.[1] Two considerations are involved: first, by refusing to begin *ab ovo* Blake intends to indicate the cyclical aspect of his story; second, he will depict the creation within the creation: the world and man come into existence only as Job acknowledges the divinity within.

God is at the centre of the design, kneeling upon a dark cloud that forms an arch separating him from Job, his wife, and the three friends who are below, all of them looking upward from what appears to be a cave, that notable symbol of confinement where 'man has closed himself up, till he sees all things thro' narrow chinks of his cavern'.[2] Clearly God, with his right foot protruding from his garment, has performed the acts of creation engraved in the two vertical borders. Immediately beneath God's arms are classical figures:[3] no doubt the figure on God's right is Apollo and that on the left Diana, as Damon suggests, and as sun and moon are representative of light, God's purest creation. The expression on God's face is serious, fervent, powerful: very much like that of Job himself, though Job by comparison to God is somewhat diminished and clearly humble.

Job is also kneeling, but his left rather than right foot protrudes from his garment. Whether this is to suggest that he is the counterpart of God, or that he is not yet fully re-created on the circle of destiny, is a question that cannot be answered with confidence. But examination of the design inclines me to the second view, for Job's right hand is raised in an incomplete gesture of prayer.

The two angels of the right and left upper borders now make their reappearance, leaning upon their familiar corners of the blank margin, having been absent since Illustration X. Each of these angels has a right hand upon a scroll—the spirit being given life. The motto across the top of the upper border is one of God's utterances after his appearance from the whirlwind. The motto is illustrated in that the angel on the left is regarding the stars of the Pleiades, and the angel on the right looks at the three stars which form the band of Orion.[4] In the lower border, the rough waters no doubt indicate the fury of creation, especially as they seem to be overwhelming a quite large and scaly serpent, and a worm twisted closely round what looks to be a wave.[5] Evil, for Blake, is part of the creation, but it is not central,[6] and therefore appears in the border rather than within the design.

---

[1] In the view of Wicksteed and also of Damon the composition of this design suggests the fourfold man and thus a vision of wholeness (Wicksteed, pp. 168-9; Damon, p. 38).

[2] *The Marriage of Heaven and Hell* (E 39, K 154).

[3] Damon, p. 38. However the reader may decide to interpret these figures he is not, I think, entitled to associate them, as Hagstrum does, with the creative figures of Los and Enitharmon in Blake's myth. Cf. Hagstrum, p. 134.

[4] The row of angels is extended, by implication, beyond the Illustration, on account of the arms and wings extended by angels not within the design. These additional angels, or rather the indications of them, are missing from the Butts, the Linnell, and the New Zealand water-colours.

[5] Damon says the worm is 'coiled round a shrouded corpse' (Damon, p. 38). Wicksteed discerns 'the flames and foaming abyss of Time and Space in which the worm and the dread serpent roll' (Wicksteed, pp. 171-2).

[6] Keynes remarks the signature that appears beneath a pencil sketch for this design: 'the words *done by* followed by a series of symbols: (1) a straight line, the simplest figure with a natural limit, i.e., immortality; (2) a hand; (3) a B, *i.e.*, Blake; (4) an eye; (5) a circle, *i.e.*, symmetry. This indicates Blake's belief that this drawing, the climax of a supreme effort, was created by the Poetic Genius in his own person.' (*Blake Studies*, pp. 148-9.) The sketch is reproduced as Pl. 34 of that volume.

15

Can any understand the spreadings of the Clouds
the noise of his Tabernacle

Also by watering he wearieth the thick cloud
He scattereth the bright cloud also it is turned about by his counsels

Of Behemoth he saith. He is the chief of the ways of God
Of Leviathan he saith. He is King over all the Children of Pride

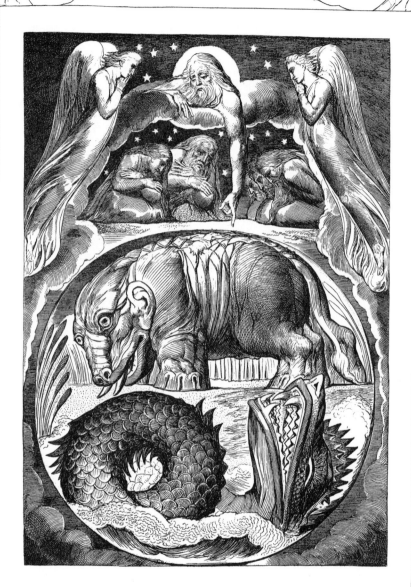

Behold now Behemoth which I made with thee

W.Blake invenit & sculpt

London Published as the Act directs March 8. 1825 by Will Blake N.s Fountain Court. Strand.

XV Behemoth and Leviathan

Leaning forward upon a cloud God points downward[1] to a globe—the circle of destiny itself,[2] which includes Behemoth, 'chief of the ways of God', and Leviathan, 'King over all the Children of Pride', the fearful symmetry of the one inescapably related to the materiality of the other. Leviathan's scaly length is coiled, and the waters are agitated; by contrast Behemoth—with an awe-inspiring human ear—is standing stock-still. Even these terrifying creatures have been 'made', and are seen to be in alliance if the doors of perception are open.[3] In contrast to the portentous meaning which these creatures bear in the Book of Job, Blake causes even hippopotamus and crocodile to be clarifyingly related to human destiny.[4] On either side of the haloed God floats an angel, hands pressed palms together. Stars form a background and establish a relationship extending to Job, his wife, and the friends, all of whom are free of the cave, but still somewhat confined, again by clouds.

Instead of the spirits on the right and upper left margins there are old and bearded though still spiritual figures, wings formed above their shoulders, leaning with their backs against the vertical margins. Both are writing upon tablets, and the engraved texts in the vertical borders suggest that these are recording angels, preparing the book for Illustration XVI. In the lower left and right corners of the margins are two eagles, upside down. The relevant text here, though it is not engraved in the borders, is: 'Doth the eagle mount up at thy command, and make her nest on high?'[5] The eagles[6] look as though they are being held back, to be released at God's command. At the bottom of the lower border in opposite corners appear two shells. Perhaps they are, as Damon remarks, 'symbols of the mortal body, which is grown by the soul for self-protection, and then discarded and left empty on the shores of the Sea of Time and Space'.[7] In addition a rather irregular-shaped cloud is drawn across the lower border, and it may be that beneath it is depicted a storm: 'Who hath divided a water course for the overflowing of waters, or a way for the lightning of thunder?'

---

[1] Damon calls attention to the similarity between the God of this design and Urizen in the frontispiece to *Europe* (Damon, p. 40).

[2] Damon calls this the sphere of the subconscious, 'the unredeemed portion of the psyche' (Damon, p. 40).

[3] Hagstrum has a more elaborate interpretation. The circle of Nature is depicted here, he says, 'not, as in the Bible, to overawe human weakness and teach sublime resignation, but to show that there is no hope in material nature as it is—a round ball filled with two monsters of warlike power, a Babylonish realm of war by land (the Behemoth) and war by sea (the Leviathan)' (Hagstrum, p. 134). He cites *Jerusalem* in support of his argument, but the evidence seems to have little bearing on the Illustration itself. Professor Percival calls Illustration XV 'perhaps the finest of all Blake's comments on the philosophy of materialism. In it we have not only his ironic criticism of a belief in corporeality but also his deeper conviction that in the scheme of salvation all such erroneous beliefs become by their very embodiment instru-

ments of their own destruction.' (Percival, p. 270.) I prefer the incarnational view, although Professor Percival can support his by reference to *Jerusalem* also.

[4] A fine gloss of the Biblical text appears in Rudolf Otto's *The Idea of the Holy*, trans. John W. Harvey (2nd ed., London, 1950), p. 80. Otto argues that Behemoth and Leviathan 'express in masterly fashion the downright stupendousness, the wellnigh daemonic and wholly incomprehensible character of the external creative power; how, incalculable and "wholly other", it mocks at all conceiving.' This interpretation throws into high relief the contrast between Blake's version of the Job story and his Biblical source.

[5] Job 39:27.

[6] Damon identifies them with those sent forth by Urizen (Damon, p. 40). Wicksteed says they are symbols of light and air (Wicksteed, p. 174).

[7] *Dict.* 363. Wicksteed declares that the shells 'express . . . the coil of revolving and evolving life' (Wicksteed, p. 174).

16

Hell is naked before him & Destruction has no covering

Canst thou find out the Almighty to perfection.

Canst thou by searching find out God

The Accuser of our Brethren is Cast down
which accused them before our God day & night

It is higher than Heaven what canst thou do

It is deeper than Hell what canst thou know

The Prince of this World shall be cast out

Even the Devils are Subject to Us thro thy Name. Jesus said unto them I saw Satan as lightning fall from Heaven

Thou hast fulfilled the Judgment of the Wicked

God hath chosen the foolish things of the World to confound the wise
And God hath chosen the weak things of the World to confound the things that are mighty

W Blake inv & sculp

London, Published as the Act directs March 8:1825 by William Blake N° 3 Fountain Court Strand.

XVI The Fall of Satan

'Thou hast fulfilled the Judgment of the Wicked.' These words, engraved prominently in the lower border of the Illustration, are flung by Elihu at Job in the Old Testament tale; but they apply in a fuller sense to the design now under consideration, for here it is Satan and his minions who are flung down to hell-fire, while Job and his wife look on. The flame in which Satan is encapsulated represents the evil heart which Job casts out; but the minions within the flame are Job and his wife themselves. Just as they appear in Illustration II under the aegis of Satan, so do they appear in this Illustration in similar circumstances. 'I saw Satan as lightning fall from Heaven' is engraved in the lower border here. But the Last Judgement includes rather than excludes Job and his wife. In *A Vision of the Last Judgment* Blake writes appositely: 'To be Cast out is a part of Gods design.' Again: 'Whenever any Individual Rejects Error & Embraces Truth, a Last Judgment passes upon that Individual.'[1] And after the Last Judgement comes, in Blake's theology, earthly salvation.

God sits upon his judgement seat here, a book open upon his knees, his right hand raised as he dispenses justice. His face is solemn; Job's is identical—but the position of Job points again to the establishment of an altered and now proper relationship with God. On the left side of the design Job and his wife kneel and regard the spectacle. Job's wife, her hands folded across her bosom, leans against her husband, but her face shows no terror; on the contrary she looks pleased to see Satan and his minions being expelled. Job, however, looks sorrowfully at the scene; perhaps he can see what his wife does not, that they themselves are involved in the Last Judgement. On the opposite side of the design the three friends, kneeling but at the same time rearing back in horror, watch the expulsion. They take no part in the Last Judgement; they are merely terrified: they are not falling, because they have not rejected error and embraced truth. But the two large angels, floating on either side of the design, look as though they may have had some share in the expulsion of Satan.[2]

---

[1] E 551, K 613.
[2] Damon declares that the flames in the margins 'consume the material creation' (Damon, p. 42). I prefer to think that they repeat and thus intensify the effect of the flames of the design itself.

17

He bringeth down to the Grave & bringeth up

We know that when he shall appear we shall be like him for we shall see him as He Is

When I behold the Heavens the work of thy hands the Moon & Stars which thou hast ordained, then I say, What is Man that thou art mindful of him? & the Son of Man that thou visitest him

I have heard thee with the hearing of the Ear but now my Eye seeth thee.

He that hath seen me hath seen my Father also

I & my Father are One

If you had known me ye would have known my Father also and from henceforth ye know him & have seen him

Beleive me that I am in the Father & the Father in me He that loveth me shall be loved of my Father for he dwelleth in you & shall be with you

At that day ye shall know that I am in my Father & you in me & I in you
If ye loved me ye would rejoice because I said I go unto the Father

He that loveth me shall be loved of my Father & I will love him & manifest myself unto him And my Father will love & we will come unto him & make our abode with him

And the Father shall give you Another Comforter that he may abide with you for ever Even the Spirit of Truth whom the World Cannot recieve

WBlake inv & sculp

London Published as the Act directs March 8: 1825 by William Blake N.º 3 Fountain Court, Strand.

XVII   The Vision of God

Before Job can be accepted he must be trained to see. The theme is insistent here, for the numerous texts which appear in the borders have as their common feature the injunction to look, and the principal motto—it appears in the lower border—is, 'I have heard of thee by the hearing of the ear, but now my eye seeth thee'. And yet Job is not looking at God, who stands directly above him and his wife; he stares away, into the middle distance. The vision which he has been taught, and which now at last he has learned, is inward:[1] through the vegetable glass of nature to a transcendence which—paradoxically but unmistakably—authenticates existence. The angelic figure[2] in the lower border is holding a quill and is certainly female, suggesting fulfilment, completion—and on earth, by art.

In the design itself a sober and benevolent God stands upon a cloud,[3] his right foot protruding from the skirts of his garment, his head and shoulders irradiated by a halo. Job and his wife, now at Job's right side, are kneeling. The three friends huddle with their backs to Job and his wife, almost but not quite out of the range of the beams shed by the halo-sun. The friends are frightened, their hands placed fearfully over their faces, and they are making themselves as small as possible. Only Bildad, the second friend, is looking toward—peeking at—the encounter of Job and his wife with God; the other two hide their faces. That they are beyond the power of vision which has been granted Job is underscored by the fact of their having turned their backs upon the tableau, and it is worth noting that in the Butts water-colour these three are facing in the opposite direction. But Blake unquestionably decided that the turning of the backs was the stronger way of making his statement, for in the Linnell and New Zealand water-colours the three friends are as in the engraved design.

---

[1] In his commentary on this design Wicksteed explores the paradox of the 'Divine-Humanity'. He does so by way of a consideration of the distinction Blake makes between Identity and Essence, the former being what differentiates each individual, the latter being what unites all men: Essence is God. Cf. Wicksteed, pp. 183-91, and Appendix E. In an unpublished note Edward Howell puts the matter with fine economy: 'Man is God, but is the equation reversible? God is ineffable and untranslatable, and at the same time so translatable that no one translation can ever be God. But it is an imperfect world which could never be the seat of Divinity. As a distorted mirror image this world lacks authenticity. It is the Divine Imagination which endows man with visionary insight.'

[2] Wicksteed says that the figure is Jerusalem (Wicksteed, p. 191); Damon, that she is the Comforter (Damon, p. 44). In the same place Damon also makes the point that the scroll and books in the lower border indicate a harmonious relationship between them—that is, letter and spirit are at last congruent.

[3] Wicksteed declares that God is ascending on the current of creation (Wicksteed, p. 182).

18

Also the Lord accepted Job

And my Servant Job shall pray for you

And the Lord turned the captivity of Job when he prayed for his Friends

WBlake inv & sculpt

London Published as the Act directs March 8 1825 by Will Blake N.ᵒ 3 Fountain Court Strand

XVIII Job's Sacrifice

Having learned to see, Job is now accepted. The change that has taken place is striking in that Job himself has risen in an attitude of prayer. He stands with arms outstretched before a flame[1] reminiscent of that in which Satan, together with Job and his wife, was seen to be falling in Illustration XVI. The flame's tip extends to a sun so large that two-thirds of its bulk is bisected by the margin between the design and the upper border: the light is infinite. The cruciform position of Job's arms suggests at once his new magnanimity and his willingness to sacrifice even himself for the friends who became his enemies.[2] Such an interpretation of the cross sorts precisely with that delineated in the fourth gospel. For John, the cross is, in the words of R. M. Grant, 'the way of Jesus' return to the Father. He uses the expression "to be lifted up" to signify at once the actual elevation of Jesus on the cross and his resurrection-ascension, which is one with his crucifixion. The cross is the way of life, a sign pointing to heaven.'[3] Even more remarkable is the oneness of Job and his God[4]—the apocalypse that comes about by recognizing the true nature of incarnation.

The altar before which Job prays is no doubt both Mosaic and Christian, leading to the syncretic significance of the final Illustration, the central meaning of the Book of Revelation itself. And the heart-shaped fire on top of the altar clearly alludes to the Biblical Job, for the lines engraved in the lower border appear in the chapter in which God enjoins the three friends to offer up a burnt offering, 'and my Servant Job shall pray for you'. When Job does pray he is accepted, and many favourable signs appear in the borders: ripening wheat, an open book commanding perfect charity, scrolls on each side of a palette and paints and burin, musical instruments. The key to this Illustration lies, as Professor Percival has suggested in an unpublished note, in the angelic figures:

If the seven angelic figures in II are Angels of Presence, or eyes—seven including Satan who was, in Job, such an angel—then there is a counterpart in XVIII, where the same six angels, appropriately drawn more lightly, are made seven in Christ (the heart shaped fire). The fire is not wholly light—there is still a cloud, but with more light.

Redemption is on the way.

---

[1] Wicksteed speculates that the flame symbolizes 'regenerate human will' (Wicksteed, p. 194).

[2] In *Job's Sacrifice*, a water-colour sketch reproduced as Pl. 72 in *William Blake's Illustrations to the Bible*, Job is facing forward, with his back to the altar. This is also his stance in the Butts water-colour, but in the Linnell and New Zealand series he is facing the altar as in the engraved design.

[3] R. M. Grant, *Gnosticism and Early Christianity* (New York, 1959), p. 173.

[4] In this interpretation I follow Wicksteed; Damon's interpretation is that 'God has now withdrawn from his complete manifestation as Man to the likeness of a great sun in the heavens.' (Damon, p. 46.)

19

The Lord maketh Poor & maketh Rich

He bringeth Low & Lifteth Up

who provideth for the
Raven his Food
When his young ones cry unto God.

Every one also gave him a piece of Money

Who remembered us in our low estate
For his Mercy endureth for ever

W Blake inv & sculp

London, Published as the Act directs March 8: 1825, by William Blake N 3 Fountain Court, Strand.

XIX Job Accepting Charity

Job and his wife have now learned the real meaning of charity. They can accept humbly because they have achieved the humility that follows upon κένωσις, the emptying of self-hood that is pre-requisite to the achievement of genuine sympathy; the charitableness depicted in Illustration V was false because patronizing and in fact defensive rather than the expression of brotherly love. Job and his wife are seated with slightly inclined heads, their eyes averted from the two pairs who have come to effect a reunion. These four represent 'all his bretheren, and all his sisters, and all they that had been of his acquaintance before, and did eat bread with him in his house: and they bemoaned him, and comforted him over all the evil that the Lord had brought upon him: every man also gave him a piece of money, and every one an earring of gold'.

The sky is becoming lighter. A fig tree is in full leaf above Job and his wife. The stones behind them are broken Druid masonry, marking a strong contrast to the thick wheat growing in the middle ground. Extending up the vertical borders are flourishing palms, among the fronds of which angels float upward. In the lower border roses of love are seen to be growing at the foot of one of the palms, and lilies of innocence grow at the foot of the other.[1] Two angels trailing fruit and flowers float gracefully upon clouds in the central section of the lower border. In the upper border two other angels float similarly. The various texts engraved here point to the Jesus who is merciful and sympathetic, Blake's Jesus.[2]

---

[1] Damon argues that they represent material and spiritual beauty respectively, but the traditional symbolic valuations sort better with Blake's practice elsewhere. Cf. Damon, p. 48.

[2] Compare the pencil sketch, *Every Man Also Gave Him a Piece of Money*, reproduced as Pl. 43 in *Blake's Pencil Drawings* (2nd series, London, 1956), ed. Geoffrey Keynes. Job and his wife are far less humble in the sketch. They have, as the editor says in an explanatory note, 'an almost self-righteous air'. Job and his wife are less humble also in the water-colour depiction of this subject, reproduced as Pl. 73 in *William Blake's Illustrations to the Bible*.

20

How precious are thy thoughts
unto me O God
how great is the sum of them

There were not found Women fair as the Daughters of Job

in all the Land & their Father gave them Inheritance

among their Brethren

If I ascend up into Heaven thou art there
If I make my bed in Hell behold Thou
art there

WBlake invent & sc

London Published as the Act directs March 8: 1825 by William Blake N° 3 Fountain Court Strand.

XX   Job and his Daughters

In another departure from the narrative of the Book of Job itself, Job tells his three daughters[1] the story of his life. The flanking scenes seem to show the destruction of his children;[2] directly behind is the voice from the whirlwind. The identity of features, God's and Job's, is patent. These three panels represent the matter of Illustrations III and XIII: art, so to speak, within art; and the spectrous elderly figures in the lower panels may represent two of the friends, the third being concealed from view by the bench on which Job and his daughters sit.[3] That the story of Job has been made into art is cardinally important in view of Blake's often iterated view of the primacy of art as a theological fact. 'Art', he writes in *The Laocoön*,

'is the Tree of Life.' And, in the same place, 'Christianity is Art'.[4] Fig trees grow up both vertical borders and many leaves and much fruit entwine themselves within all the borders. A pair of angels embrace on the upper left margin, and another pair seems ready to embrace in the upper right margin.

The theme of this Illustration is gracefully and accurately carried out in the circularity of the wall panels, the curve of the room, and the design of the floor.[5] The circle of Blake's Job narrative is now complete, and the regeneration has taken place. There remains only the necessity of depicting the renewal itself. This is to be the matter of the subsequent and ultimate Illustration.[6]

---

[1] Damon says that the daughters represent Poetry, Painting, and Music because in the Butts water-colour version of this scene they are holding 'instruments of their arts' (Damon, p. 50). But Blake's dissociation of such patent symbolism in the final version marks, in my view, an advance. Nor am I disposed to accept Wicksteed's ingenious speculation that the daughters may represent sun, moon, and earth because Job's attitude is similar to that of the Creator of Illustration XIV. Cf. Wicksteed, p. 205.

[2] Hagstrum interprets the panel to Job's left differently. He thinks it depicts 'a scene recalling Blake's famous representation of himself being inspired by Milton, a poet receiving the inspiration of Los. . . . Like Los defeating evil by giving it form Job the artist has transcended his experiences by shaping them, and Urizen is now imprisoned in a wall design near the floor.' (Hagstrum, p. 135.) This is ingenious but further away from the Job series than necessary, and yet Hagstrum argues it again with much force in an important essay called 'Blake's Blake', in Heinz Bluhm, ed., *Essays in History and Literature Presented . . . to Stanley Pargellis* (Chicago, 1965), pp. 174-5. Northrop Frye offers the following explanation, not of the individual panels of this Illustration, but of their status. 'These pictures are on the walls of Job's mind, for the room he is in is identical with his own body. That does not make them subjective, for Job is no longer

a subject: he is one with God.' (*Fearful Symmetry* [Princeton, N.J., 1947], p. 434.) I like this interpretation.

[3] Conclusive identification of these figures may be impossible, but I cannot agree with Damon's assertion that they are Job and his wife in despair (Damon, p. 50).

[4] E 271, K 777.

[5] Damon says that the circular shape of the floor represents 'the communion of the heaven of art; the smaller circles represent individuals entering each other's bosoms' (Damon, p. 50).

[6] A pencil sketch of *Job and His Daughters* is reproduced as Pl. 42 in *Pencil Drawings by William Blake*, ed. Geoffrey Keynes (London, 1927). And the tempera painting, now in the Rosenwald Collection at the National Gallery in Washington, is reproduced as Pl. 74 of *William Blake's Illustrations to the Bible*. In the Butts water-colour Job and his daughters are out of doors and his recital to them is depicted in a cloudlike mass above his head. God in the whirlwind and the striking Satan are also depicted. The Linnell set represents a half-way house: the depictions— very faint—are on panels on a wall, but there is grass beneath the feet of Job and his daughters, and a number of sheep lie nearby. The New Zealand series puts this scene altogether indoors.

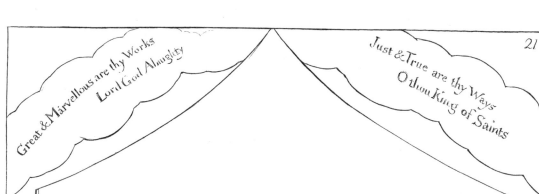

Great & Marvellous are thy Works Lord God Almighty

Just & True are thy Ways O thou King of Saints

So the Lord blessed the latter end of Job
more than the beginning

After this Job lived
an hundred & forty years
& saw his Sons & his
Sons Sons

even four Generations
So Job died
being old
& full of days

In burnt Offerings for Sin

thou hast had no Pleasure

W Blake inv & sculp

London Published as the Act directs March 8: 1825 by William Blake Fountain Court Strand

XXI Job and his Wife restored to Prosperity

Illustration XXI is the counterpart of Illustration I; the differences are underscored by the similarities. The restoration to prosperity signals not a return to the state in which Job and his family were depicted at the beginning of the story, but a renewal of the innocence that had already been lost when the story opened. Innocence and redemption are not the same, as the *Songs of Innocence and of Experience* repeatedly testify; but to sort out the differences between them is not the purpose of Blake's Job series. The important point here is that innocence is susceptible of renewal[1] and indeed must be renewed if the circle of destiny is to be completed in accordance with the highest hopes—which is to say the most exalted prophecies—of the Book of Revelation. The Biblical Job learns to accept suffering simply as a mystery. Blake's Job confronts himself and finds that he has been wanting: so he has acknowledged to his daughters in Illustration XX; already his story has been told. Now, in the last Illustration, it is history and—more important—art.

Instead of praying pietistically as in Illustration I, Job and his family are engaged here in making music, beneath the cosmic tree, symbolic now of a unity regained rather than a unity endangered. They are blowing horns, plucking lutes and harps, and some also singing. They are certainly involved in the particulars of art rather than in the abstractions of the letter that killeth. In contrast to Illustration I, the moon is seen to be setting, and now is associated with Job's wife, while the rising sun[2] is associated with Job. Again, the sheep and dog in the present Illustration are awake rather than somnolent. The lamb and the bullock of the lower border of Illustration I are now in the opposite corners to those they were at first, and the altar upon which the sacrificial lambs appear, in the central section of the lower border, now contains a new motto. And the reason why the Lord does bless the latter end of Job more than the beginning is the story told in the Job Illustrations themselves. When Job has learned to see and to understand, then the astonishing truth of the Book of Revelation comes home, the truth that the song of Moses

and the song of the Lamb are the same: it is this song whose words are engraved in the upper border of this triumphant Illustration. The force of the words is the greater for their contrast with the opening words of the Lord's Prayer which appear in the upper border of Illustration I. The putting of God at a distance, the setting off of a Father in heaven, is antipathetic to Blake's theology: 'God only Acts and Is, in existing beings or Men.'[3] And the force of the song from Revelation is the greater also when the whole verse is examined: 'And they sing the song of Moses the servant of God, and the song of the Lamb, saying Great and Marvellous are thy works, Lord God Almighty; just and true are thy ways thou King of saints.' Finally, there is an absence to be noted here: the church of Illustration I has disappeared. This is in accord with that in Revelation itself, where there is no temple. In Revelation there is simply light, inward and outward.

Nevertheless, the circle, though complete, is unfinished. The portentous dog at the centre of this Illustration makes this point. The Job series engraved by Blake at the end of a long and often difficult career provides an earned but wary triumph. It is joyful, but open-eyed. Job learned to see because Blake knew how to look. The patriarch, the artist, and we ourselves can find in such knowledge a kind of glory.

In the plate prefatory to Chapter four of *Jerusalem* Blake engraved the following words:

> I give you the end of a golden string,
>   Only wind it into a ball:
> It will lead you in at Heavens gate
> Built in Jerusalems wall.[4]

The Job Illustrations provide Blake's best and clearest telling of the tale of the way to heaven's gate. The route is by way of imaginative realization, in art. Blake writes on the same plate,

> I know of no other Christianity and of no other gospel than the liberty both of body and mind to exercise the Divine Arts of Imagination . . . O ye Religious, discountenance every one among you who shall pretend to despise Art & Science! I call upon you in the Name of Jesus. What is the Life of Man but Art & Science?

---

[1] Northrop Frye puts the matter especially well, in a comment on the differences between the first and last Job Illustrations: 'In the last plate, things are much as they were before, but Job's family have taken the instruments down from the tree and are playing them. In Blake we recover our original state, not by returning to it, but by recreating it. The act of creation, in its turn, is not producing something out of nothing, but the act of setting free what we already possess.' ('The Keys to the Gates',

in James V. Logan *et al.*, eds., *Some British Romantics* [Columbus, Ohio, 1966], p. 40.)

[2] In the Butts water-colour version, the following words are engraved in the sun: 'Great & Marvellous are thy Works   Lord God Alm   Trust & Con'. Linnell shows the same words, as far as 'Lord'.

[3] E 39, K 155. Blake is echoing Rev. 21:1-4. But Blake's utterance is more directly incarnational.   [4] E 229, K 716.

APPENDIX I

THE BIBLICAL TEXTS AND BLAKE'S ALTERATIONS

All the Biblical texts are identified by chapter and verse. In the 'Collation' column such differences as exist between the words engraved by Blake and those in the Authorized Version are indicated. Occasionally also a fuller biblical context is provided. When nothing appears under 'Collation' the Biblical quotation is virtually identical to that in the engraving and provision of a wider Biblical context appears to be unnecessary.

BIBLE	BLAKE ILLUSTRATION	CATCHWORDS	COLLATION
Matt. 6: 9	I	Father	[A.V. After this manner therefore pray ye:] Our Father which art in Heaven hallowed be thy Name
Job 1: 5	I	Job	[A.V. And it was so, when the days of their feasting were gone about that Job sent and sanctified them, and rose up early in the morning and offered burnt offerings according to the number of them all: for Job said, It may be that my sons have sinned, and cursed God in their hearts.] Thus did Job continually
Job 1: 1–2	I	Land of Uz	There was a man in the Land of Uz whose Name was Job & that Man was perfect & upright & one that feared God & eschewed Evil & there was [A.V. were] born unto him Seven Sons and Three Daughters
2 Cor. 3: 6	I	Killeth	[A.V. Who also hath made us able ministers of the new testament; not of the letter, but of the spirit, for] The Letter Killeth [A.V. but] The Spirit giveth Life
1 Cor. 2: 14	I	Spiritually	[A.V. But the natural man receiveth not the things of the spirit of God: for they are foolishness unto him: neither can he know them because] It is [A.V. they are] Spiritually Discerned
Dan. 7: 9	II	Ancient of Days	I beheld [A.V. till the thrones were cast down, and] the Ancient of Days [A.V. did sit, whose garment was white as snow, and the hair of

53

BIBLE	BLAKE ILLUSTRATION	CATCHWORDS	COLLATION
			his head like the pure wool: his throne was like the fiery flame, and his wheels as burning fire.]
Job 1: 8	I I	considered	[A.V. And the Lord said unto Satan] Hast thou considered my Servant Job [A.V. that there is none like him in the earth, a perfect and an upright man, one that feareth God, and escheweth Evil?]
Isa. 64: 8	I I	Thou art	[A.V. But now, O Lord,] Thou art our Father [A.V. we are the clay and thou our potter; and we all are the work of thy hand]
Ps. 17: 15	I I	awake	[A.V. As for me, I will behold thy face in righteousness] We shall awake up in thy Likeness [A.V. I shall be satisfied, when I awake, with thy likeness]
Job 29: 5	I I	Almighty	
Job 2: 1	I I	Sons of God	[A.V. Again] There was a day when the Sons of God came to present themselves before the Lord & Satan came also among them to present himself before the Lord.
Job 19: 26	I I	see God	[A.V. And though after my skin worms destroy this body, yet in my flesh] I shall [A.V. shall I] see God
Isa. 63: 9	I I	Angel	[A.V. In all their affliction he was afflicted, and] The Angel of the Divine [A.V. his] Presence [A.V. saved them: in his love and in his pity he redeemed them; and he bare them and carried them all the days of old.]
Job 1: 16	I I I	Fire	[A.V. While he was yet speaking, there came also another, and said] The Fire of God is fallen from Heaven [A.V. and hath burned up the sheep, and the servants, and consumed them; and I only am escaped alone to tell thee.]
Job 1: 12	I I I	Behold	And the Lord said unto Satan Behold All that he hath is in thy Power [A.V. only upon himself put not forth thine hand. So Satan went forth from the presence of the Lord]

BIBLE	BLAKE ILLUSTRATION	CATCHWORDS	COLLATION
Job 1: 18–19	III	Wine	[A.V. While he was yet speaking, there came also another, and said] Thy Sons & Thy Daughters were eating & drinking Wine in their eldest Brothers house & behold there came a great wind from the Wilderness & smote upon the four faces [A.V. four corners] of the house & it fell upon the young Men & they are Dead [A.V. and I only am escaped to tell thee]
Job 1: 14–15	IV	Sabeans	And there came a Messenger unto Job & said The Oxen were plowing [A.V. and the asses feeding beside them] & the Sabeans came down & [A.V. fell upon them and took them away; yea,] they have slain the Young Men [A.V. the servants] with the Sword [A.V. with the edge of the sword] and I only am escaped alone to tell thee.
Job 1: 7, 2: 2	IV	To & Fro	[A.V. And the Lord said unto Satan, Whence comest thou? Then Satan answered the Lord, and said, From] Going to & fro in the Earth & [A.V. from] walking up & down in it
Job 1: 16	IV	Fire of God	While he was yet speaking there came also another & said The Fire of God is fallen from heaven & hath burned up the flocks [A.V. sheep] & the Young Men [A.V. the servants] & consumed them & I only am escaped alone to tell thee
Job 30: 25	V	weep	Did I not [A.V. Did not I] weep for him who [A.V. that] was in trouble Was not my Soul afflicted [A.V. grieved] for the Poor
Job 2: 6	V	Behold	[A.V. And the Lord said unto Satan,] Behold he is in thy [A.V. thine] hand: but save his Life
Job 2: 7	V	presence	Then [A.V. So] went Satan forth from the presence of the Lord [A.V. and smote Job with sore boils from the sole of his foot unto his crown]
Gen. 6: 6	V	grieved	[A.V. And it repented the Lord that he had made man on the earth,] And it grieved him at his heart

BIBLE	BLAKE ILLUSTRATION	CATCHWORDS	COLLATION
Ps. 104: 4	V	Angels	Who maketh his Angels Spirits and [A.V. omits and] his Ministers a Flaming Fire
Job 1: 21	VI	Naked	[A.V. And said] Naked came I out of my mothers womb & Naked shall I return thither. The Lord gave & the Lord hath taken away. Blessed be the Name of the Lord
Job 2: 7	VI	Boils	[A.V. So went Satan forth from the presence of the Lord] And smote Job with sore Boils from the sole of his foot to the [A.V. unto his] crown of his head [A.V. omits of his head]
Job 2: 10	VII	What!	[A.V. But he said unto her, Thou speakest as one of the foolish women speaketh] What! shall we recieve Good at the hand of God & shall we not also [A.V. omits also] recieve Evil [A.V. In all this did not Job sin with his lips.]
Job 2: 12	VII	lifted up	And when they lifted up their eyes afar off & knew him not they lifted up their voice & wept. & they rent every Man [A.V. one] his mantle & sprinkled dust upon their heads towards heaven
Jas. 5: 11	VII	Patience	Ye have heard of the Patience of Job and have seen the end of the Lord [A.V. that the Lord is very pitiful, and of tender mercy.]
Job 3: 7	VIII	solitary	Lo let that night be solitary & [A.V. omits and] let no joyful voice come therein
Job 3: 3	VIII	perish	Let the Day perish wherein I was Born [A.V. and the night in which it was said, There is a man child conceived.]
Job 2: 13	VIII	sat down	And [A.V. So] they sat down with him upon the ground seven days & seven nights & none spake a word unto him for they saw that his grief was very great
Job 4: 17	IX	mortal	
Job 4: 18, 15: 15	IX	Behold	Behold he putteth [A.V. put] no trust in his Saints [A.V. servants] and his Angels he chargeth [A.V. charged] with Folly Behold he putteth no trust in his Saints [K.J. omits from 'and his Angels' and adds: yea, the heavens are not clean in his sight.]

BIBLE	BLAKE ILLUSTRATION	CATCHWORDS	COLLATION
Job 4: 15	IX	Spirit	
Job 23: 10	X	knoweth	But he knoweth the way that I take when he hath tried me I shall come forth like [A.V. as] gold
Job 19: 21	X	pity	
Job 13: 15	X	slay	Though he slay me yet will I trust in him [A.V. but I will maintain mine own ways before him.]
Job 12: 4	X	Upright	[A.V. I am as one mocked of his neighbour, who calleth upon God, and he answereth him] The Just Upright Man is laughed to scorn
Job 14: 1–3	X	Woman	Man that is born of a Woman is of few days & full of trouble he cometh up [A.V. forth] like a flower & is cut down he fleeth also as a shadow & continueth not And dost thou open thine eyes upon such a [A.V. an] one and bringest me into judgment with thee
Job 30: 17	XI	bones	
Job 30: 30	XI	skin	
Job 20: 5	XI	triumphing	[A.V. That] The triumphing of the wicked is short, the [A.V. and the] joy of the hypocrite is [A.V. omits is] but for a moment
2 Cor. 11: 14–15	XI	Satan	[A.V. And no marvel; for] Satan himself is transformed into an Angel of Light and [A.V. omits and] [Therefore it is no great thing if] his Ministers into [A.V. also be transformed as the] Ministers of Righteousness
Job 7: 13–14	XI	Dreams	[A.V. When I say, My bed shall comfort me, my couch shall ease my complaint] With Dreams upon my bed thou scarest me & affrightest me [A.V. Then thou scarest me with dreams and terrifiest me] with [A.V. through] Visions
Job 19: 22–7	XI	persecute	Why do you [A.V. ye] persecute me as God & are not satisfied with my flesh Oh that my words were [A.V. now written! oh that they

BIBLE	BLAKE ILLUSTRATION	CATCHWORDS	COLLATION
			were] printed in a Book that they were graven with an iron pen and lead in the rock forever For I know that my Redeemer liveth & that he shall stand in [A.V. at] the latter days [A.V. day] upon the Earth & [A.V. though] after my skin [A.V. *adds* worms] destroy thou [A.V. *omits* thou] This body, yet in my flesh shall I see God whom I shall see for Myself and mine eyes shall behold & not Another tho consumed be my wrought Image [A.V. though my reins be consumed within me.]
2 Thess. 2: 4	XI	opposeth	Who opposeth and exalteth himself above all that is called God or [A.V. that] is Worshipped
Job 33: 14	XII	speaketh	For God speaketh once yea twice and [A.V. yet] Man percieveth it not
Job 33: 15	XII	Vision	In a Dream in a Vision of the Night [A.V. when deep sleep falleth upon men,] in deep Slumberings upon the bed
Job 33: 16	XII	openeth	
Job 33: 17	XII	withdraw	
Job 33: 23	XII	Interpreter	If there be [A.V. a messenger] with him an Interpreter One among a Thousand [A.V. to shew unto man his uprightness]
Job 33: 24	XII	Ransom	
Job 34: 21	XII	eyes	For his eyes are upon the ways of Man & he observeth [A.V. seeth] all his goings
Job 32: 6	XII	Young	[A.V. And Elihu the son of Barachel the Buzite answered and said] I am Young and ye are very Old wherefore I was afraid [A.V. and durst not shew you mine opinion.]
Job 33: 29-30	XII	pit	
Job 35: 5	XII	heavens	Look upon [A.V. unto] the heavens [A.V. and see;] and behold the clouds which are higher than thou
Job 35: 6-7	XII	sinnest	If thou sinnest what doest thou against him [A.V. or if thy transgressions be multiplied,

BIBLE	BLAKE ILLUSTRATION	CATCHWORDS	COLLATION
			what doest thou unto him] or [A.V. *omits* or] if thou be righteous what givest thou unto [A.V. *omits* unto] him [A.V. or what receiveth he of thine hand?]
Job 38: 2	XIII	darkeneth	
Job 38: 1	XIII	Whirlwind	
Ps. 104: 3	XIII	Clouds	[A.V. Who layeth the beams of his chambers in the waters:] who maketh the Clouds his Chariot & [A.V. who] walketh on the Wings of the Wind
Job 38: 28	XIII	Rain	Hath the Rain a Father & [K.J. *omits* and] who hath begotten the Drops of the [A.V. *omits* the] Dew
Job 38: 31	XIV	Pleiades	
Gen. 1: 3	XIV	Light	[A.V. And God said] Let there Be Light [A.V. and there was light]
Gen. 1: 6	XIV	Firmament	[A.V. And God said] Let there be A Firmament [A.V. in the midst of the waters, and let it divide the waters from the waters.]
Gen. 1: 9	XIV	Waters	[A.V. And God said] Let the Waters [A.V. under the heaven] be gathered together unto one place & let the Dry Land appear [A.V. and it was so]
Gen. 1: 16	XIV	Great Lights	And God made Two Great Lights [A.V. the greater light to rule the day, and the lesser light to rule the night: he made the stars also] Sun Moon [A.V. *omits* sun *and* moon]
Gen. 1: 20	XIV	abundantly	[A.V. And God said] Let the Waters bring forth abundantly [A.V. the moving creature that hath life, and fowl that may fly above the earth in the open firmament of heaven.]
Gen. 1: 24	XIV	Earth	[A.V. And God said] Let the Earth bring forth [A.V. the living creature after his kind] Cattle & Creeping thing & Beast [A.V. of the earth after his kind: and it was so.]
Job 38: 7	XIV	morning Stars	

BIBLE	BLAKE ILLUSTRATION	CATCHWORDS	COLLATION
Job 36: 29	X V	understand	[A.V. Also] Can any understand the spreadings of the Clouds [A.V. or] the noise of his Tabernacle
Job 37: 11-12	X V	watering	Also by watering he wearieth the thick cloud He scattereth the [A.V. his] bright cloud also [A.V. and] it is turned [A.V. round] about by his counsels [A.V. that they may do whatsoever he commandeth them upon the face of the world in the earth.]
Job 40: 19	X V	Behemoth	Of Behemoth he saith [A.V. *omits the foregoing words*] He is the chief of the ways of God [A.V. he that made him can make his sword to approach unto him.]
Job 41: 34	X V	Leviathan	Of Leviathan he saith [A.V. *reads*: He beholdeth all high things] He is [A.V. a] King over all the Children of Pride
Job 40: 15	X V	Behold	Behold now Behemoth which I made with thee [A.V. he eateth grass as an ox.]
Job 26: 6	X V I	Hell	Hell is naked before him & Destruction has [A.V. hath] no covering
Job 11: 7	X V I	searching	Canst thou by searching find out God Canst thou find out the Almighty to [A.V. unto] perfection
Rev. 12: 10	X V I	Accuser	[A.V. And I heard a loud voice saying in heaven, now is come salvation and strength, and the kingdom of our God, and the power of his Christ: for] The Accuser of our Brethren is Cast down which accused them before our God day & night
Job 11: 8	X V I	higher	It is higher than [A.V. as high as] Heaven what canst thou do It is [A.V. *omits* it is] deeper than Hell what canst thou know
John 12: 31	X V I	Prince	[A.V. Now is the judgment of this world: now shall] The Prince of this World shall [A.V. *omits* shall] be cast out
Job 36: 17	X V I	fulfilled	[A.V. But] Thou hast fulfilled the Judgment of the Wicked [A.V. judgment and justice take hold on thee]

BIBLE	BLAKE ILLUSTRATION	CATCHWORDS	COLLATION
Luke 10: 17-18	XVI	Devils	[A.V. And the seventy returned again with joy, saying, Lord] Even the Devils are Subject to [A.V. unto] Us thro thy Name. Jesus [A.V. and he] said unto them I saw [A.V. beheld] Satan as lightning fall from Heaven
1 Cor. 1: 27	XVI	foolish	[A.V. But] God hath chosen the foolish things of the World to confound the wise And God hath chosen the weak things of the World to confound the things that [A.V. which] are mighty
1 Sam. 2: 6	XVII	Grave	[A.V. The Lord killeth, and maketh alive] He bringeth down to the Grave & bringeth up
1 John 3: 2	XVII	appear	[A.V. Beloved, now are we the sons of God, and it doth not yet appear what we shall be, but] We know that when he shall appear we shall be like him for we shall see him as He Is
Ps. 8: 3-4	XVII	Heavens	When I behold [A.V. consider] the [A.V. thy] Heavens the work of thy hands [A.V. fingers] the Moon & [A.V. the] Stars which thou hast ordained then I say [A.V. *omits* then I say] What is Man that thou art mindful of him? & the Son of Man that thou visitest him
Job 42: 5	XVII	heard	I have heard thee [A.V. of thee] with [A.V. by] the hearing of the Ear but now my [A.V. mine] Eye seeth thee
John 14: 9	XVII	seen	[A.V. Jesus saith unto him, Have I been so long time with you, and yet hast thou not known me, Philip?] He that hath seen me hath seen my [A.V. the] Father also [A.V. *omits* also]
John 10: 30	XVII	my Father	
John 14: 7	XVII	known	If you [A.V. ye] had known me ye would [A.V. should] have known my Father also and from henceforth ye know him & have seen him
John 14: 11	XVII	Believe	Believe me that I am in the Father & the Father in me

BIBLE	BLAKE ILLUSTRATION	CATCHWORDS	COLLATION
John 14: 21	XVII	loveth	[A.V. He that hath my commandments and keepeth them, he it is that loveth me: and] He that loveth me shall be loved of my Father [A.V. and I will love him, and will manifest myself to him.]
John 14: 17	XVII	dwelleth	[A.V. Even the Spirit of truth; whom the world cannot receive, because it seeth him not, neither knoweth him: but ye know him] For he dwelleth in [A.V. with] you & shall be with [A.V. in] you
John 14: 20	XVII	day	At that day ye shall know that I am in my Father & you [A.V. ye] in me & I in you
John 14: 28	XVII	loved	If ye loved me ye would rejoice because I said I go unto the Father [A.V. for my Father is greater than I]
John 14: 21	XVII	manifest	[A.V. He that hath my commandments and keepeth them, he it is that loveth me and] He that loveth me shall be loved of my Father & I will love him & [A.V. will] manifest myself unto him
John 14: 23	XVII	abode	[A.V. Jesus answered and said unto him, If a man love me he will keep my words] And my Father will love him & we will come unto him & make our abode with him
John 14: 16	XVII	Comforter	And the Father [A.V. And I will pray the Father and he] shall give you Another Comforter that he may abide with you forever
John 14: 17	XVII	Spirit	Even the Spirit of Truth whom the world cannot recieve [A.V. because it seeth him not, neither knoweth him: but ye know him; for he dwelleth with you and shall be in you.]
Job 42: 9	XVIII	accepted	[A.V. So Eliphaz the Temanite and Bildad the Shuhite and Zophar the Naamathite went, and did according as the Lord commanded them] Also the Lord [A.V. the Lord also] accepted Job
Job 42: 8	XVIII	Servant	[A.V. Therefore take unto you seven bullocks and seven rams, and go to my servant Job,

BIBLE	BLAKE ILLUSTRATION	CATCHWORDS	COLLATION
			and offer up for yourselves a burnt offering] And my Servant Job shall pray for you [A.V. for him will I accept: lest I deal with you after your folly, in that ye have not spoken of me the thing which is right, like my servant Job.]
Job 42: 10	XVIII	captivity	And the Lord turned the captivity of Job when he prayed for his Friends [A.V. Also the Lord gave Job twice as much as he had before.]
Matt. 5: 44	XVIII	bless	[A.V. But] I say unto you Love your Enemies bless them that curse you do good to them that hate you and pray for them that [A.V. which] despitefully use you & persecute you
Matt. 5: 45	XVIII	children	That you [A.V. ye] may be the children of your Father which is in heaven, for he maketh his sun to shine [A.V. rise] on the Evil & [A.V. on] the Good & sendeth rain on the Just & [A.V. on] the Unjust
Matt. 5: 48	XVIII	perfect	Be ye therefore perfect [A.V. even] as your Father which is in heaven is perfect.
1 Sam. 2: 7	XIX	Poor	
Job 38: 41	XIX	provideth	who provideth for the Raven his Food When his young ones cry unto God
Job 42: 11	XIX	Money	[A.V. Then came there unto him all his brethren, and all his sisters, and all they that had been of his acquaintance before, and did eat bread with him in his house: and they bemoaned him and comforted him over all the evil that the Lord had brought upon him] Every one [A.V. man] also gave him a piece of Money [A.V. and everyone an earring of gold.]
Ps. 136: 23	XIX	Mercy	
Ps. 139: 17	XX	precious	How precious [A.V. also] are thy thoughts unto me O God how great is the sum of them
Job 42: 15	XX	Women	There were not found Women fair as the Daughters of Job in all the Land [A.V. And

BIBLE	BLAKE ILLUSTRATION	CATCHWORDS	COLLATION
			in all the land were no women found so fair as the daughters of Job] & their Father gave them Inheritance among their Brethren
Ps. 139: 8	XX	Heaven	
Rev. 15: 3	XXI	Marvellous	[A.V. And they sing the song of Moses, the servant of God, and the song of the lamb, saying] Great & Marvellous are thy Works Lord God Almighty Just & True are thy Ways O [A.V. *omits* O] thou King of Saints
Job 42: 12	XXI	blessed	So the Lord blessed the latter end of Job more than the [A.V. his] beginning [A.V. for he had fourteen thousand sheep, and six thousand camels, and a thousand yoke of oxen, and a thousand she asses]
Job 42: 16	XXI	hundred	After this Job lived [A.V. lived Job] an hundred & forty years & saw his Sons & his Sons Sons even four Generations
Job 42: 17	XXI	Full of days	
Heb. 10: 6	XXI	Offerings	In burnt Offerings [A.V. and sacrifices] for Sin thou hast had no Pleasure

APPENDIX II

PREVIOUS STUDIES OF THE JOB ILLUSTRATIONS

JOSEPH WICKSTEED'S *Blake's Vision of the Book of Job* was first published in 1910 and it has affected every subsequent commentary. In fact, two of the great pioneers of modern Blake scholarship—Wicksteed himself and S. Foster Damon—learned from each other: in writing *William Blake, His Philosophy and Symbols* (Boston, Mass., 1924), Damon was able to employ Wicksteed's many findings; and in revising his commentary for the expanded second edition of *Blake's Vision of the Book of Job* (London, 1924) Wicksteed drew upon Damon. Of the particularities of this reciprocal indebtedness something must be said by way of some general remarks on each work in turn.

The advantage—and also the disadvantage—of Wicksteed is his exhaustiveness. In his eagerness to consider every detail he occasionally misses the wood for the trees—and so, almost inevitably, does his reader. Occasionally too his enthusiasm carries him beyond the edge of the horizon, as when he writes of the 'mysterious kinship' of Illustration XVII and the Beethoven sonata Opus 111. But his every judgement and *aperçu* must be carefully weighed, so resourceful is his approach, so thorough and supple is his knowledge of Blake's work.

Wicksteed was perhaps not the first to observe that Blake's Job Illustrations offer an interpretation of the Biblical tale that differs considerably from its source, but he was the first to act on this observation. In his endeavour to relate the Illustrations to Blake's system, he applies with great assiduity an interpretation of the symbolism of the series whereby right and left stand for spiritual and material respectively: 'by this device he [Blake] really intended to express in every design something quite definite and often quite argumentative and polemical' (p. 14). A further symbolic interpretation relates the clockwise direction (to be observed for instance in the movement of the angels of the title-page) to what Blake calls the 'current of creation'. Thirdly, Wicksteed argues that the inner and outer worlds are to be distinguished by the use of the cloud belt throughout the series, the two worlds being differentiated according to a principle enunciated in *Jerusalem*: 'What is Above is Within' (Plate 71, line 6— E 222, K 709). Above all, Wicksteed considers the Job Illustrations to possess a four-fold structure, leading to the fourfold vision—the complete vision of the whole man that Blake had celebrated in his well-known letter to Thomas Butts of 22 November 1802. Thus Wicksteed writes:

> The work . . . divides itself symmetrically . . .: i.–vi. Job loses the things of the earth; vii.–xi., Job loses the things of heaven; xii.–xv., Job, by the help of Elihu, recovers the things of earth in a new vision;

xvi.-xxi., Job discovers the things of heaven in the eternal vision. In the first Act he loses all he possesses, even his children, and in a sense his wife. In the second Act his own religion and that of his friends is revealed as utter destruction of soul. In the third Act Elihu opens his eyes to the glory of the outside universe displayed in the three following illustrations. But only a fourth Act can complete the theme. God may be found even in Nature, but it is within and not in the outward order that his true being dwells. This can only be known after a Last Judgment, which is the rejection of Error, and thus Illus. 16 opens the way to a Paradise through Christ (pp. 74-5).

S. Foster Damon's commentary on the Job Illustrations has made four appearances. The first is Chapter 30 of *William Blake, His Philosophy and Symbols*. Much of this chapter is reprinted, with minor variations, as 'William Blake's Doctrine of Job' in an edition of the Illustrations issued in New York in 1947, with an introductory note by Kenneth Patchen. A considerably revised version appears in Damon's *Blake Dictionary* (Providence, R.I., 1965), s.v. 'Job', and—again revised—in his *Blake's Job* (Providence, R.I., 1966). While making generous acknowledgement to Wicksteed for the discovery of the symbolism of right and left, Damon discerns a different over-all structure of the series. Taking the seven angels of the title-page as his point of departure, he discovers a sevenfold arrangement throughout, the seven angels, or eyes, representing

respectively Pride in the Selfhood; the Executioner; the Judge; the Accuser; Horror at the results; the Perception of Evil; and finally the Revelation of the Good. This is Man's customary course through Experience. Blake devotes two plates to each in turn; then, the climax having been reached, the order is reversed, the final plate ending where the first began. These last seven plates show, as might be expected, the same impulse, or 'Eye', in its redeemed aspect (p. 224).

The structural apprehension is elaborated in a chart in the 1966 edition of the Illustrations: besides the sevenfold division two further divisions are discerned, a threefold cycle (Illustrations I-VII, VIII-XIV, and XV-XXI), and a structure reflecting five states (Innocence, I-II; Experience, III-VII; Revolution, VIII; The Dark Night, IX-XI; and The New Life, XII-XXI). To me such proposed divisions are less helpful than particular comments on details of the Illustrations themselves; to such comments I make repeated reference in the Notes.

The third study of great importance is of a different sort: the edition of *The Illustrations of the Book of Job* by Laurence Binyon and Geoffrey Keynes (New York, 1935). The interpretation offered follows Wicksteed; what is important here is the informed commentary on the differences among the several versions of the Job series preceding that of the engraved designs. The 134 plates in this lavish edition are well reproduced and must be studied by any one interested in the genesis of the Illustrations. Sir Geoffrey's *Blake Studies* (London, 1949) contains two chapters bearing on Job; they are revised versions of chapters appearing in the 1935 edition.

Jean H. Hagstrum's *William Blake: Poet and Prophet* (Chicago, 1964) contains a brief but useful appreciation of the Job Illustrations, especially from the viewpoint of their relationship to Blake's art and to the artistic tradition within which he worked. In this fine study Professor Hagstrum builds on the contribution made by Sir Anthony Blunt in *The Art of William Blake* (New York, 1959), though Sir Anthony offers little new in the way of interpretation of the Job Illustrations. In 'Blake's Reading of the Book of Job', published in *William Blake: Essays for S. Foster Damon*, edited by Alvin H. Rosenfeld (Providence, R.I., 1969), Northrop Frye argues that Blake 'clearly saw in the story of Job . . . a microcosm of the whole biblical story'. It is a fine essay.

General studies of Blake, whether biographical or critical, often have something to say about Blake's Job; all but two or three of these commentaries repeat what Wicksteed and Damon have said. Such is the case, for instance, in the still standard *Life of William Blake* by Mona Wilson (3rd edition, London, 1948); Miss Wilson makes no claims to originality in her remarks on this subject. Exceptional insights, however, are provided by M. O. Percival in *William Blake's Circle of Destiny* (New York, 1938) and by Northrop Frye in *Fearful Symmetry* (Princeton, N.J., 1947), though neither author attempts detailed analysis of the Job Illustrations themselves. Throughout the present volume I have taken account of the earlier commentaries—I have learned much from them— and I have recorded alternative interpretations in the notes.